EDGAR CAYCE ON ESP

by Doris Agee
under the editorship of
Hugh Lynn Cayce

PAPERBACK LIBRARY

New York

PAPERBACK LIBRARY EDITION
First Printing: May, 1969

*Paperback Library is a division of Coronet Communications,
Inc. Its trademark, consisting of the words "Paperback Library"
accompanied by an open book, is registered in the United States
Patent Office.* Coronet Communications, Inc., 315 Park Avenue
South, New York, N.Y. 10010.

CONTENTS

Out of the wealth of material in the Cayce files grew the Association for Research and Enlightenment, Inc., and its affiliated organizations, the A.R.E. Press and the Edgar Cayce Foundation.

The Foundation is engaged in the complicated task of indexing and cross-indexing the hundreds of subjects discussed in the readings. Because of their age, the papers are rapidly deteriorating, and they are now being microfilmed for safekeeping and duplicated for ready reference. The subject matter almost blankets the field of human thought; from the value of peanuts to the building of the Great Pyramid; from how to get rid of pinworms to prophecy of the future.

The Association for Research and Enlightenment is an open-membership, nonprofit organization chartered under the laws of the Commonwealth of Virginia to carry on psychic research. It is devoted to the study of the readings and conducts numerous experiments in psychic phenomena. It also cooperates in the fields of medicine, psychology and theology. The active membership of the A.R.E., as it is usually called, is made up of people of all religious faiths and many nationalities, including foreign countries. Strangely, they all seem to be able to reconcile their faiths with the philosophy emerging from the Cayce readings. They come from all walks of life; there are doctors, lawyers, ministers, artists, businessmen, teachers, students, working people, housewives.

The Association, governed by a board of trustees, conducts conferences at the Virginia Beach headquarters and regional conferences in New York, Dallas, Denver, Los Angeles and other large cities.

The Association and its affiliated organizations occupy a large, rambling, three-story frame building of shore architecture. Standing on the highest elevation at Virginia Beach, the building and grounds take up a full city block and face the Atlantic Ocean, a block away. A new building has been constructed which houses a lecture hall, classrooms, offices and the A.R.E. Press.

Hundreds of visitors come every year. With the steadily growing membership and interest, a growing staff handles volumes of inquiries, special requests, lecture announcements and literature. Visitors are shown about the plant and grounds with its broad, tiled veranda overlooking the ocean. The library containing indexed copies of 90% of the readings is of special interest.

To the skeptic there is an appropriate answer: in the words of Abraham Lincoln, "No man has a good enough memory to be a successful liar!" for forty-three years.

INTRODUCTION

WHO WAS EDGAR CAYCE?

The twelve books which have been written about Edgar Cayce have totaled more than five million in sales. Many other books have devoted sections to his life and talents. He has been featured in dozens of magazines and hundreds of newspaper articles dating from 1900 to the present. What was so unique about him?

It depends on through whose eyes you look at him. A goodly number of his contemporaries knew the "waking" Edgar Cayce as a gifted professional photographer. Another group (predominantly children) admired him as a warm and friendly Sunday School teacher. His own family knew him as a wonderful husband and father.

The "sleeping" Edgar Cayce was an entirely different figure—a psychic known to thousands of people, in all walks of life, who had cause to be grateful for his help. Indeed, many of them believed that he alone had either saved or changed their lives when all seemed lost. The "sleeping" Edgar Cayce was a medical diagnostician, a prophet, and a devoted proponent of Bible lore.

In June, 1954, the University of Chicago held him in sufficient respect to accept a Ph.D. thesis based on a study of his life and work. In this thesis the writer referred to him as a "religious seer." In that same year, the children's comic book *House of Mystery* bestowed on him the impressive title of "America's Most Mysterious Man!"

Even as a child, on a farm near Hopkinsville, Kentucky, where he was born on March 18, 1877, Edgar Cayce displayed powers of perception which seemed to extend beyond the normal range of the five senses. At the age of six or seven he told his parents that he was able to see and talk to "visions," sometimes of relatives who had recently died. His parents attributed this to the overactive imagination of a lonely child who had been influenced by the dramatic language of the revival meetings which were popular in that section of the country. Later, by sleeping with his head on his schoolbooks, he developed some form of photographic memory which helped him advance rapidly in the country school. This gift faded, however, and Edgar was only able to complete his seventh grade before he had to seek his own place in the world.

By the age of twenty-one he had become the salesman for a wholesale stationery company. At this time he developed a gradual paralysis of the throat muscles which threatened the loss of his voice. When doctors were unable to find a physical cause for this condition, hypnosis was tried, but failed to have any permanent effect. As a last resort, Edgar asked a friend to help him re-enter the same kind of hypnotic sleep that had enabled him to memorize his schoolbooks as a child. His friend gave him the necessary suggestion, and once he was in a self-induced trance, Edgar came to grips with his own problem. He recommended medication and manipulative therapy which successfully restored his voice and repaired his system.

A group of physicians from Hopkinsville and Bowling Green, Kentucky, took advantage of his unique talent to diagnose their own patients. They soon discovered that Cayce only needed to be given the name and address of a patient, wherever he was, to be able to tune in telepathically on that individual's mind and body as easily as if they were both in the same room. He needed, and was given, no other information regarding any patient.

One of the young M.D.'s, Dr. Wesley Ketchum, submitted a report on this unorthodox procedure to a clinical research society in Boston. On October 9, 1910, *The New York Times* carried two pages of headlines and pictures. From that day on, troubled people from all over the country sought help from the "wonder man."

When Edgar Cayce died on January 3, 1945, in Virginia Beach, Virginia, he left well over 14,000 documented stenographic records of the telepathic-clairvoyant statements he had given for more than six thousand different people over a period of forty-three years. These documents are referred to as "readings."

The readings constitute one of the largest and most impressive records of psychic perception ever to emanate from a single individual. Together with their relevent records, correspondence and reports, they have been cross-indexed under thousands of subject headings and

8

placed at the disposal of psychologists, students, writers and investigators who still come, in increasing numbers, to examine them.

A foundation known as the A.R.E. (Association for Research and Enlightenment, Inc., P.O. Box 595, Virginia Beach, Virginia, 23451) was founded in 1932 to preserve these Readings. As an open-membership research society, it continues to index and catalog the information, initiate investigation and experiments, and promote conferences, seminars and lectures. Until now, its published findings have been made available to its members through it's own publishing facilities.

This new book was designed to discuss the question, "What are the varieties of ESP which can be found in the records of Edgar Cayce's work?"

Doris Agee has brought to this material not only a writing style of clarity and directness of a good reporter but also the intellectual intensity of a research-minded seeker. She is obviously fascinated by the mechanics of the Edgar Cayce readings. Her opening chapters will help answer for many readers the oft heard questions, "Why was *he* able to do it?" and "How were the readings given?"

Presenting new cases for the most part, Mrs. Agee opens up a bewildering area of ESP capacities in the Edgar Cayce data. She uses the physical and life readings as sources of telepathic-clairvoyant insight. Her section on missing persons presents some cases which have never been examined before. Her treatment of scientific confirmation of many of the prophecies is very well handled.

In all this is a welcome addition to the series of new books on the Edgar Cayce readings.

—*Hugh Lynn Cayce*

CHAPTER ONE

"THE UNIVERSAL MIND"

Until a few years ago, only the most foolhardy of men would openly acknowledge his belief in the existence of "sixth sense," that enigmatic something we now generally call extrasensory perception, or ESP. To admit acceptance of such an idea was to court criticism, derision and in some extreme cases a suspicion that one had lost his reason.

For the unconscious mind is a dark, mysterious place. Many centuries passed before man became convinced that he *had* an unconscious mind, operating on many different levels; and then many more years went by before he began to feel that he had a right to investigate its workings.

Not that humanity has ever suffered a dearth of psychic phenomena! How many "witches" were drowned or burned at the stake before man came to understand that just because something could not be explained by established scientific law, it wasn't necessarily evil? How many people who experienced true psychic phenomena were judged insane and put behind locked doors, simply because other people couldn't accept the truth of what had happened?

We've come a long way in the past few decades. We've now reached the point where individuals are publicly discussing ESP and psychic phenomena and asking questions about the subject. It is no longer a question of, "Do I believe in ESP?" Rather, more and more people are asking, "Now that I know that ESP exists, how can I learn more about it? How does it work? Do I have it? If I develop my own ability to use it, will it harm me or help me?"

Many of the answers to these and other questions may be found in the remarkable collection of psychic readings given by an outstanding clairvoyant, Edgar Cayce, during the more than forty years of his adult life. Although much has been written about Cayce, the scope of his psychic ability and of the subjects he treated while in a self-imposed hypnotic sleep are so vast that great portions of the knowledge they contain are still, as yet, untapped.

It is the purpose of this book to present to the reader, mainly through use of the readings themselves, material which may aid his understanding of psychic phenomena as well as the individual's own place and value in today's troubled world.

Cayce's own psychic abilities enabled him to help many thousands of people; but in many ways they brought terrible burdens to his own life. Often misunderstood by his contemporaries, he went out of his way to make his "waking" hours seem as ordinary and commonplace as those of every other man. Throughout his life he was constantly being tested and challenged, sometimes under severe physical pain, because people simply couldn't believe he could do the things they'd heard he could do. On several occasions he was jailed as a fraud, accused of cheap showmanship or of practicing medicine without a license. None of these claims were valid; he was a quiet, humble man who supported a wife and children more on faith than money.

A common reaction, upon first learning of the work of Edgar Cayce, is to think of his clairvoyant abilities as something in the nature of magic. Edgar Cayce's own description of it, as shown in the many readings he gave on the subject, is much more down to earth. Later chapters will go into this in more detail, but a general explanation might be in order here.

As the readings explained it, the knowledge gained while Cayce was in a self-induced sleep came principally from the subject's *own* unconscious mind. He was, in effect, simply "tuning in" to the correct frequency.

He described the levels or degrees of an individual's unconscious mind, and he talked about the collective unconscious in which the individual unconscious has its origin. This collective, or universal, unconscious he described as a vast "river" of thought flowing through eternity, fed by the collective mental activity of mankind since its beginning. According to Cayce, this collective unconscious is accessible to anyone who develops his own psychic faculties to such a degree as to be able to draw from, as well as feed into, this river of thought.

This was nothing new, really. Scholars and philosophers since ancient times have advanced similar theories about the unconscious mind. But Edgar Cayce didn't just *tell* about it; he *performed* it. His highly developed psychic abilities put theory into practice, with information that has been proved accurate again and again.

The story of Edgar Cayce is remarkable in two important ways. First, of course, is the extraordinary scope of his psychic powers, his extrasensory perception. Second, and equally important, is the fact that meticulous records were kept of the readings he gave during his lifetime, and these have been carefully maintained and *used* in the more than two decades since his death. Over 14,000 readings, and a large number of studies based on their contents, are completely indexed and available to interested researchers. These are living files in every sense of the word, for they contain vast amounts of knowledge that may be used by this generation, and many generations to come, in man's never-ceasing struggle to understand himself and the world he inhabits.

Edgar Cayce has been called the Miracle Man of Virginia Beach. It is an understandable and apt title. Although the readings reflect, at first glance, the realization of Cayce's boyhood dream to someday help people, as he certainly did with the thousands of physical and life readings he gave, they contain much, much more.

They contain, for example, a great deal of the history of man—some of which may have passed, for the moment, out of the realm of accepted knowledge. If so, future archaeological findings may confirm many of the events Cayce spoke of in his readings. This has already happened in some instances.

One such example followed the discovery of the Dead Sea Scrolls in 1947 by two shepherd boys grazing their goats in the vicinity of Khirbet Qumran. Cayce, in giving a life reading for a woman in 1936, had referred to her having been, in a previous incarnation, a Sister Superior in an Essene community. At the time of the reading it was believed that only men had inhabited such communities. But in 1951 excavations into ruins near the coast of the Dead Sea established the fact that an Essene monastery had existed just where Cayce had placed it in his reading.

12

And when graves surrounding the community were opened, skeletons of many women were found!

Cayce was a deeply religious man. Thus it was a moving experience for him when, in the course of a reading given spontaneously, he seemed to "attend" the Last Supper. He described it in detail, and it will be presented, just as he told it, in a later chapter.

Edgar Cayce "read" the past, but he also read the future, both for individuals and for mankind as a whole. For instance, he predicted both world wars, and furnished the dates of beginning and ending. He predicted the stock market crash of 1929, the gradual lifting of the depression beginning in 1933, racial violence in America (pinpointed with absolute accuracy as to the time it would begin), and talked of the death in office of two presidents (Roosevelt and Kennedy, although he did not name them). These and other Cayce prophecies will be discussed in a separate chapter on the subject.

He read the present. As will be illustrated throughout the following pages, Cayce's ability to put his own unconscious mind in complete communication with the unconscious minds of others was, by accepted definition, telepathic in nature; that is, he read the conscious or unconscious thoughts and ideas of others. But much of it was also clairvoyant; he was able to acquire knowledge of physical objects or events (apart from mental ones) without the use of any of the recognized channels of communication. These were abilities within his power to control. Although some of his psychic experiences were spontaneous, most of them occurred because he *willed* them to occur. For example, he might experience a dream during the course of a normal night's sleep. What set him apart, however, was that he could later put himself to sleep deliberately and ask for, and receive, an interpretation of what he had dreamed! Even more remarkable, if his conscious memory of the dream was dim, his unconscious memory of it would fill in any missing details at the time the interpretation was going on! Some of his dream interpretations, as well as his explanation of what might be considered universal dream symbols, will be explored in a later chapter.

Edgar Cayce also, at times, participated in *conscious*

psychic phenomena. Visions came to him all through his life; he experienced his first one at the age of six. As with his dreams, he was able to gain, via the psychic readings, interpretations of his visions; and often his source of information would supply the answer to the question, "Was the experience had by Edgar Cayce on such-and-such a date a dream, or a vision?"

Another interesting talent of his was the ability to see, when looking at any individual, an aura: a kind of halo of light and color which told him much about the mental and physical well-being of the person he was consciously viewing. This will be discussed later in this book, together with some special color charts developed by Cayce: a sort of do-it-yourself-analyze-your-friends kit.

When giving a reading, he seemed actually to put himself where the subject of the reading was situated—even if that person was halfway around the world. The Cayce files are full of indications of his awareness, during the readings, of physical surroundings and actions of the person receiving the reading.

Once a Hopkinsville, Kentucky, businessman, doubting Cayce's ability to do all the things he'd heard about, challenged Cayce to trace his steps as he went from his home to his office on a particular day. Cayce, who had a high regard for skeptics, accepted the challenge. At the appointed hour, in the office of the local newspaper, Cayce put himself to sleep.

The man went out of his way to trick him. He altered his usual route. Instead of buying the single cigar in the tobacco store at which he stopped each morning, this time he purchased two. He took the stairway to his second floor office instead of the elevator. But when he arrived at his office, he put the "test" out of his mind and went about his daily business, beginning with opening and reading the morning mail.

Many people in Hopkinsville were highly amused to learn that Cayce had "seen" him every step of the way. But he was amazed, and a little disconcerted, to discover that Cayce had also read his mail!

Once, at the beginning of a reading, Cayce exclaimed, "Yes, not bad looking pajamas!" A check with the patient later got the response that he had wanted to make sure

Edgar Cayce would be able to "find" him, so he had deliberately put on a pair of new pajamas—bright red ones at that.

Another time, after repeating the location of the subject in an undertone, Cayce said, "Yes, we have had this place before." A check through the files showed that, although this particular subject had not had a reading previously, his brother-in-law had, several months before. Both men had been at the home of the brother-in-law when their readings were given.

One day Cayce put himself into trance easily enough, but then seemed a little reluctant to begin the reading; he showed signs of having been distracted by something. Then he said, "1075 Park Avenue. Very unusual in some of these halls, isn't it? What funny paintings!" He then went on with the reading as if there were nothing out of the ordinary. A query about this to the subject brought the response that there were some very unusual wall adornments in the hall, including some wood plaques from Central America. At the time of the reading, however, she had been neither looking at them nor thinking about them.

Often the readings would begin with such statements as, "Yes, little stream there . . ." or, "That's a right pretty tree on the corner!"

It seems that Cayce, while giving a reading, was always aware of what the person was doing at the time. Once he began with the usual, "Yes, we have the body here." Then he raised his voice a little, saying, "It would be better if he would keep quiet a minute. No use bawling *that* man out!" A check with the subject later brought a somewhat chastened admission that he had been shouting at one of his employees at the time set for the reading.

Normally, only one physical reading was given at a session. However, follow-up readings—called check readings—were usually brief, and often they were scheduled so that Cayce could do several while in the same hypnotic sleep. He wasn't told the names of the subjects in advance; these were given only at the beginning of each individual reading. John Brewer, scheduled for a reading at nine thirty, stayed in his Baltimore apartment until ten o'clock, as he'd told the Cayce office he would do. At that time, he began making preparations to leave for his office. At precisely the same time, at Virginia Beach, Edgar Cayce was being given the suggestion to read for a San Francisco man. Suddenly he interrupted the proceedings. "Better take John Brewer first. He's going out!" The readings were switched. A follow-up with Brewer later confirmed that this is exactly what had happened.

Throughout the files, there are many indications that Edgar Cayce not only "saw" the subjects of his readings and their surroundings but knew, as well, what people were doing. Thus we find a great many statements such as:

"Come back here and sit down!"

"Yes, we have the body here. The body is just leaving, going down in the elevator now."

"Out for the walk and coming in now."

Once he located the subject of a reading on a Fifth Avenue bus. The man had been held up in traffic, and was still en route to the appointed location. Edgar Cayce, giving the reading from his home in Virginia Beach, mentioned that the subject was not at the New York location given in the reading suggestion, and then proceeded to do a little psychic detective work by tracking down the man. Once the subject was in Cayce's "view," the reading went off without a hitch.

Often Cayce would correct information given to him at the beginning of the reading. Once Gertrude Cayce identified the subject by her nickname, rather than her given name as used in an earlier reading. Edgar Cayce said, "Yes, we have the body here. This we have had before. Different names, same body." (This, incidentally, is a striking example of the phenomenal memory shown by Cayce when in the sleeping state. No matter how many years elapsed between readings, he never seemed to forget anything and simply picked up where the other reading had left off!)

Another time, after the location of the subject had been furnished by him, Edgar Cayce said, "We do not find the body here, but rather at the office—11th and Virginia Street." The subject, when asked about this later, replied that at the time of the reading she had been in her office, at the address Cayce had supplied, rather than at home as originally planned.

16

In addition to the readings given for diagnosing and prescribing treatment for physical problems, Edgar Cayce gave many of a type called "life readings." These dealt mainly with psychological problems, vocational talents, personal characteristics, and so forth, examined in the light of what Edgar Cayce called the "karmic patterns," arising out of previous lives spent on the earth by the individual soul (called, by Cayce, "the entity").

The life reading began with a suggestion different from that used in the physical reading. That is, instead of identifying the individual by name and present location, as used in obtaining physical readings, the conductor of the life reading furnished Cayce with the name, birth date and location of birth of the subject. (The hour of birth was also helpful to Cayce; if the subject couldn't supply this, Cayce often would.) To get his psychic information on the subject, the sleeping Cayce would consult what he referred to as "the book." When he found what he was looking for, he'd say, "Yes, we have the record."

Apparently subjects could keep no secrets from Cayce. One day a life reading suggestion was given for a young woman born January 23, 1919, at Mount Sinai Hospital in New York City. This information had been supplied by the subject before the reading. When Cayce began, however, he said, "We don't find it here. Yes, we have the record here (looks like it's the wrong place and date) of that entity now known as or called Martha Smith." The subject's mother finally got things straightened out by advising the Cayce office that her daughter didn't have it exactly right; she had been born, in fact, on January 24, 1919, in Cleveland, Ohio. The subject was quite dismayed to learn that Cayce knew about this, when she herself did not!

One striking example of Cayce's clairvoyant powers is shown in a life reading he gave for a man born in a town in Texas on February 25, 1906. In locating the "record" for this man, Cayce said of the town, "Quaint place! Not too nice a day, either, is it?" This reading was given on August 21, 1944. A check with the weather bureau in the Texas town showed that the weather, pleasant for several days just prior to February 25, 1906, had suddenly turned extremely warm and uncomfortable that day. Cayce had not only located the town in question, he'd gone back in time some thirty-eight years and given a weather report on it!

Whenever a statement of this type was made by Cayce during the course of a reading, the Cayce office would contact the subject for confirmation or denial of its accuracy. Not all the subjects responded, of course, but in some forty-three years of readings, no one ever notified the office that such a statement "just wasn't so."

Now let's examine, in detail, the way Edgar Cayce went about his business of "helping people."

A Kind of Miracle

Outside, at four o'clock in the afternoon of a day in October, 1940, the air was cold and crisp. Inside, in the small examining room of a Kentucky hospital, the air was stifling, and filled with the terrible sound of a child's screaming.

The cause of the screaming was all too apparent. The child, a little girl just one year old, lay naked on the white table. From her blonde hairline to her toes, nearly every inch of skin that could be seen was deeply scalded, the result of a container of boiling water she'd pulled down on herself half an hour earlier. With over fifty percent of her skin surface involved, the doctors didn't hold out much hope for her survival. Even if she lived, they admitted to each other—although not yet to the young parents—she'd most likely be badly scarred, and quite possibly blind.

They waited, now, for the results of a telephone call the child's father had just made to Edgar Cayce's home at Virginia Beach. The answers would come soon. Because the doctors had experienced such telephone calls in the past, and knew the good that could come from them, they'd agreed to go along with whatever they were instructed to do.

The parents waited, too, in the small hospital room. The child's father looked at his watch and said softly, "It's time." Then he took his wife's hand, and together they moved away from the child and sat down in the two straight chairs by the window. Silently, they lowered their heads in prayer.

18

Eight hundred miles away, Edgar Cayce was getting ready to perform what some called a kind of miracle. He was going to put himself to sleep, and while he was asleep he was going to describe in detail what was wrong with the child, and what to do for her—this child he had never seen. He didn't even know it *was* a child. All he knew was that a telephone call had just come in, requesting a emergency reading for someone, and that he was going to try to get "the information"—he always called it this—necessary to help that person.

In truth, he didn't look like the sort of man who could perform miracles. He was thin and quite tall, which probably accounted for the slight stoop to his shoulders. He was sixty-three years old and his hairline, as well as his chin, receded a little. If there was anything mystical about his appearance, it was in the large, blue-gray eyes that peered from behind rimless spectacles with a brilliant intensity.

Now he sat on the edge of the couch and untied his shoes, removed his tie, and unbuttoned his collar and cuffs; it was important that there be nothing binding. He swung his long legs onto the couch and lay back quietly. He smiled at his wife, Gertrude, who was to "conduct" the reading, and at his secretary of many years, Gladys Davis, who would note in shorthand precisely what he said, for he would remember none of it afterwards. He placed his hands on his forehead and closed his eyes. His breathing gradually deepened. He moved his hands to his abdomen, and began to breathe normally. Now he seemed to be simply taking an afternoon nap.

Gertrude said the words to begin the reading, just as she had said them so many times before. She told him only the name and present location of the patient, leaving out any mention of age, sex, or physical problem. Then she said, "You will give the physical condition of this body at the present time, with suggestions for further corrective measures, answering the questions as I ask them."

Edgar Cayce lay silent for several moments. Then he began to mumble, in a strange, faraway voice, repeating the name and location of the child to himself several times. Suddenly he cleared his throat, and spoke in a voice

19

that was clear and forceful, that carried more authority than his waking voice.

"Yes," he said. "We have the body here. While these appear very serious in the present, because of the blister or the water, we do not find the injury to the eyes, but rather to the lids."

He then proceeded to outline, step by step, the treatment to be used by the doctors to heal the skin. "We would cleanse and use the tannic acid, followed with the Unguentine and the camphorated oil to prevent or remove scars, as the tissue heals.

"Be very mindful that eliminations are kept above the normal. Use *both* the Podophyllum and the calomel as a base for eliminants, at various times, not together. But under the direction of the physician. While these would not be used under most circumstances for a child, these would be the better in this case—because of the poisons from so much area covered with the burn, and the shock to the system, as well as the kind of poisons to be eliminated, and the need for the excess lymph.

"Ready for questions."

Gertrude Cayce asked, "Apply tannic acid?"

The answer came quickly. "Tannic acid; the light, to be sure. This is understood by the physician. Cleanse it first, then apply the tannic acid."

"How should it be cleansed?"

With a note of scorn, Edgar Cayce replied, "Would you ask how to tell a doctor to cleanse a thing!"

"Are they using the tannic acid in the way suggested here?"

"Not using it as yet, but it should be a part of the bandages."

The strange dialogue continued between the sleeping man and his wife.

"Then after the tannic acid apply the Unguentine?"

"As it heals. Not, of course, while the tannic acid is being used, but as it heals. See, this cuts away air, produces dead skin, and leaves a scar. Then the oils from the Unguentine, and the camphorated oil, are to take away scar tissue, see? These are to follow within ten days to two weeks, see?"

"The eyes themselves are not injured?"

"As indicated, the lids; though there will be, of course, some inflammation. But keep down the excesses of poisons by increasing the eliminations, to remove these poisons that are as natural accumulations from such an area burned."

"Any suggestions for relieving the pain?"

"As just given, this will relieve the pain when it cuts off the air!"

Gertrude needed no further clarification, and Edgar Cayce ended the reading as he always did, by saying, "We are through for the present."

Doctors caring for the little girl applied the tannic acid bandages as prescribed by Cayce. They had never used this method before, but as a result of this case and its outcome, added it to the regimen for many such burn cases with excellent results. They balked, at first, at the idea of administering such strong eliminants for a baby, but finally agreed to go along with Cayce's reading on an "all or nothing" basis.

Twelve days later, a second reading was given for the child. Cayce announced that ". . . improvements have been rather phenomenal . . ." as far as healing of the skin was concerned. This time, his major concerns were lowering the fever and helping the body get rid of excess fluids and toxic substances that were accumulating faster than the kidneys could dispose of them—often a cause of death in severe burn cases. His instructions dealt with removing these fluids with certain eliminants; on this occasion he gave exact dosages to be used. He also prescribed gentle spinal massages twice a day with a mixture of one part grain alcohol to two parts water to reduce the fever; this was possible because the child's back was practically the only portion of her body not burned in the accident. He gave specific advice on the diet, and repeated his earlier instructions for applying Unguentine and camphorated oil to prevent the formation of scar tissue.

The child's recovery was complete. However, when she was three years old she was given another reading in which Cayce was asked to prescribe something to remove, or lessen, the one scar remaining on her arm. He recommended frequent massage with a mixture of two ounces of camphorated oil, one-half teaspoon dissolved lanolin, and one ounce peanut oil. (This, incidentally, is a Cayce "invention" which was prescribed in a number of cases. It has been used by many people, with various types of scars, who have found it quite effective.)

Now twenty-eight, this young woman is walking proof of what Cayce's readings could do when followed in every detail. She has no scars from a burn so severe it could have killed her. Indeed, she is exceptionally beautiful, and only the fact that she is married, and the mother of three handsome sons, keeps her from working as a photographer's model, which she has often been invited to do. Her eyesight? She doesn't need glasses even for reading!

CHAPTER TWO

WHAT IS A READING?

It is most fortunate that, among the many thousands of readings given by Edgar Cayce during his lifetime, a large number were devoted to the subject of psychic phenomena. People—including Cayce himself—wanted to know what, exactly, he did when he put himself into trance. And how he got the information he got. And from what source. And why. So they asked him, and the sleeping Cayce replied.

We live in a world that demands scientific proof of such phenomena before any of it may be accepted. So Cayce's answers, for the time being at least, must be considered theory, rather than fact.

But what an interesting theory they form!

Cayce's Conscious Description

One of the clearest statements on the Cayce work was made by Edgar Cayce himself in an address to a study group on February 6, 1933. He began:

"What is a reading?

"It is rather hard to describe something which has become so much a part of me—almost like trying to describe what my face looks like. I can show you, but I can't tell you. I might tell you some of my experiences and thoughts concerning the readings; but as to what a reading is I can only tell you what others have said about them and what has come to me as I have studied the effect created in the minds of those receiving readings.

"It would not be an exaggeration to say that I have been in the unconscious state (during which the readings are given) perhaps twenty-five thousand times in the last thirty-one years; yet I myself have never heard a single reading. How can I describe one to you?

"Many people who have never heard a reading have asked me just how I knew I could give one. I never did know it—don't know it yet—except by taking another person's word for it.

23

"The first step in giving a reading is this: I loosen my clothes—my shoelaces, my necktie, my shirtcuffs, and my belt—in order to have a perfectly free-flowing circulation.

"Then I lie down on the couch in my office. If the reading is to be a physical one, I lie with my head to the south and my feet to the north. If it is to be a life reading, it is just the opposite: my feet are to the south, my head to the north. The reason for this difference is 'polarization,' as the readings themselves call it. I do not know.

"Once lying comfortably, I put both hands up to my forehead, on the spot where observers have told me that the third eye is located, and pray. Interestingly enough, I have unconsciously and instinctively, from the very beginning, adopted the practices used by initiates in meditation. This instinctive putting of my hands to the point midway between my two eyes on my forehead is a case of what I mean.

"Then I wait for a few minutes, until I receive what might be called the 'go signal'—a flash of brilliant white light, sometimes tending towards the golden in color. This light is to me the sign that I have made contact. When I do not see it, I know I cannot give the reading.

"After seeing the light I move my two hands down to the solar plexus, and—I'm told—my breathing now becomes very deep and rhythmic, from the diaphragm. This goes on for several minutes. When my eyes begin to flutter closed (up until now they have been open, but glazed) the conductor knows I am ready to receive the suggestion, which he proceeds to give me, slowly and distinctly. If it is a physical reading, for example, the name of the individual to receive the reading is given me, together with the address where he will be located during that period of time. There is a pause—sometimes so long a pause, they tell me, that it seems I haven't heard the directions, so they give them to me again—after which I repeat the name and address very slowly, until the body is located, and a description of its condition is begun.

"This, then, is how I give a reading. I am entirely unconscious throughout the whole procedure. When I wake up I feel as if I had slept a little bit too long. And frequently I feel slightly hungry—just hungry enough for a cracker and a glass of milk, perhaps.

"As to the validity of the information that comes through me when I sleep—this, naturally, is the question that occurs to everyone. Personally, I feel that its validity depends largely on how much faith or confidence the one seeking has in the source of information. Of course its validity has been objectively proved many hundreds of times by the results that have come from applying the advice.

"With regard to the source of information, I have some ideas, naturally; but even though I have been doing this work for thirty-one years I know very little about it. Whatever I could say would be largely a matter of conjecture. I can make no claim whatsoever to great knowledge. I, too, am only groping.

"But then, we all learn only by experience. We come to have faith or understanding by taking one step at a time. We don't all have the experience of getting religion all at once, like the man who got it halfway between the bottom of the well and the top when he was blown out by an explosion of dynamite. We all have to have our experiences and arrive at conclusions by weighing the evidence with something that responds from deep within our inner selves.

"As a matter of fact, there would seem to be not only one, but several sources of information that I tap when in this sleeping condition.

"One source is, apparently, the record that an individual or entity makes in all its experiences through what we call time. The sum total of the experiences of that soul is "written," so to speak, in the subconscious of that individual as well as in what is known as the akashic records. Anyone may read these records if he can attune himself properly.

"Apparently I am one of the few who can lay aside their own personalities sufficiently to allow their souls to make this attunement to this universal source of knowledge—but I say this without any desire to brag about it. In fact, I cannot claim to possess anything that other individuals do not inherently possess. Really and truly, I do not believe there is a single individual who doesn't possess this same ability I have. I am certain that all human beings have much greater powers than they are ever conscious of—if they would only be willing to pay the price of detachment from self-interest that it takes to develop those abilities. Would you be willing, even once a year, to put aside, pass out entirely from, your own personality?

"Some people think that the information coming through me is given by some departed personality who wants to communicate with them, or some benevolent spirit or physician from the other side. This may sometimes be the case, though in general I am not a 'medium' in that sense of the term. However, if a person comes seeking that kind of contact and information, I believe he receives it.

"Many people ask me how I prevent undesirable influences entering into the work I do. In order to answer that question, let me relate an experience I had as a child.

"When I was between eleven and twelve years of age I had read the Bible through three times. I have now read it fifty-six times. No doubt many people have read it more times than that, but I have tried to read it through once for each year of my life. Well, as a child I prayed that I might be able to do something for the other fellow, to aid others in understanding themselves, and especially to aid children in their ills. I had a vision one day which convinced me that my prayer had been heard and would be answered.

"I still believe that my prayer is being answered and as I go into the unconscious condition I do so with that faith. So I believe that if the source is not wavered by the desires of the individual seeking the reading, it will be from the universal.

"Of course if an individual's desire is very intense to have a communication from Grandpa, Uncle, or some great soul, the contact is directed that way, and that becomes the source. Do not think that I am discrediting those who seek in that way. If you're willing to receive what Uncle Joe has to say, that's what you get. If you're willing to depend on a more universal source, that's what you get. 'What ye ask ye shall receive' is a two-edged sword. It cuts both ways."

Thus we have Cayce's own conscious description of his

work. Many of the points he touched on in his talk will be expanded in succeeding chapters.

Earlier, in a reading given in 1923, Edgar Cayce reported that psychic readings were not new. "Among the Chaldeans they were first used as the means of assistance to physical bodies—not in the same manner as they are given today. They came as the *natural* means of expression of an unseen force; the soul and spirit of an earthly individual, manifesting through the physical body, enabled that life-giving flow of such revelations to appear—nearly four thousand years before the Prince of Peace came."

Language of the Readings

Before we embark on what Edgar Cayce, in his readings, had to say about psychic matters in general, and his own psychic work in particular, we must pause for a moment and consider the peculiar language he spoke while in the sleeping state. It is, at times, difficult.

Anyone who has researched the readings to any degree has been frustrated, sooner or later, by the strange phraseology, the complicated sentence structure, the allusions and circumlocutions of the Cayce language. Gina Cerminara, who has written so much about Edgar Cayce, authored a witty treatise on this subject in the April, 1966, A.R.E. *Journal*.

"Why," she wondered, "did he have to engage in psychic double talk? Why, instead of saying, 'This is a spade,' did he have to say something such as, 'This as we find has to do with not the consciousness in spirituality (as commonly conceived) but rather the consciousness of materiality, as condensed in what is known as, or called, in the present, an implement of spading, or a spade.' "

Portions of the readings do sound as obscure as Dr. Cerminara's made-up example—although we will not boggle your mind with them in this book, but will paraphrase when necessary.

At times, no doubt the people working closest to Edgar Cayce were frustrated by the language, too. A gentle hint of this is found in a reading given in April, 1934, wherein Cayce was asked, "Are there any suggestions or counsel that may be given at this time that will aid in securing

27

clearer, more valuable information?"

Cayce seems to have evaded them rather neatly. He replied, "Seek and ye shall find. As given, that which may be helpful and hopeful on any subject that pertains to the welfare of the souls and bodies of individuals may be sought through these channels . . ."

Even earlier than that, however, those working with Cayce asked him outright, in a reading given in April, 1932, "How can the language used in the readings be made clearer, more concise and more direct?"

"Be able to understand it better!" he said.

There is much valuable and interesting material in what Cayce had to say, however awkwardly some of it may seem to be worded. If you would "be able to understand it better," then, do take time to read and reread difficult portions. Just as you found when you first encountered Shakespeare or Chaucer, familiarity with the particular "shape" of the language will make you more comfortable with it.

CHAPTER THREE

SOURCES OF EDGAR CAYCE'S INFORMATION

As we have mentioned, the readings themselves named two major sources of information available to the sleeping Cayce. There are indications of other sources as well.

The First Source

This was the unconscious mind of the person for whom the reading was being given. Edgar Cayce, in putting his conscious mind out of the way and letting his unconscious mind take over, by means of self-induced hypnosis, was able to "tune in" on the unconscious mind of the individual.

In view of what we now know about the workings of the unconscious mind, this seems quite acceptable. No one pretends to understand the mechanics of such an accomplishment, but there are many thousands of Cayce readings, dealing with the diagnosis and suggested treatment for physical disorders of all types, that can hardly be explained in any other way. One thing is certainly clear: whatever it was that Cayce was doing, it worked—and it worked extremely well.

What *are* some of the things we know about the unconscious mind? Well, for one thing, we know that it is fed by the conscious mind, which has in its turn been fed by the five recognized senses of sight, hearing, taste, touch and smell. We know that the unconscious mind never forgets. And we know that it can receive messages given so quickly that the conscious mind is not even aware of them; experiments with subliminal advertising have shown this to be true. We know that a hypnotherapist can say to a receptive subject under hypnosis, "I am burning your arm with a red hot poker," and touch the arm with any object at all, and a blister will form in that spot. We know, then, that the subconscious mind exerts tremendous control over the physical body. We know that the hypnotherapist can put his subject into varying levels of sleep all the way from an almost-conscious state to a sleep so deep that the subject will respond to no stimulus whatsoever. We know that each level of sleep seems to have its own memory track. Something told the subject at Level A, for example, might not be recalled at Level D, but will be recalled verbatim when the subject is brought back to Level A again.

We know that the subconscious mind speaks a literal language. The hypnotherapist can say, "Can you give me your date of birth?" and the unconscious mind, speaking through the subject, will reply, "Yes." The unconscious mind will not reply to such a question with the birthdate, but will merely indicate that it *can* reply if it wants to!

Yes, we know a lot about the unconscious mind. But there's a great deal we don't know about it. We don't know, as yet, just how deep it may go, and we still don't know quite how it works. We don't know what principle governs the peculiar tie-up between the will of the hypnotherapist and the willingness of the unconscious mind of a receptive subject to comply with correctly worded commands. Most of what we now know of the unconscious mind has come directly from experimentation with the process of hypnosis.

But the subject of a Cayce reading was not under hypnosis. He might have been half a world away when Cayce reached out psychically and put his own unconscious mind in tune with that of his subject. And while today's hypnotherapist, working within the framework of accepted medical procedure, is concerned only with taking the subject's unconscious mind back as far as earliest childhood, Cayce went much further. He went deep into the subject's unconscious and "read" the history of that person's past lives!

Cayce's first experience with this phenomenon, in a reading given in 1923, shocked and dismayed him, for it seemed to be in direct opposition to his orthodox Christian beliefs and training. Over a period of more than twenty years, he had given many thousands of psychic readings dealing with physical problems. Now the same informational source was indicating that people spend many lifetimes on earth. Even more startling was the indication that they carry the unconscious memory of these lifetimes with them into each new appearance on the earth—and

Edgar Cayce had been given the means of telling them about it! This seemed incredible to Cayce, and he wanted no part of it.

Had his physical readings not been proven accurate and useful in all the years he had been giving them, he probably would have turned from this new development in his psychic work and never have given another reading of any kind. Fortunately, however, he decided—after much soul-searching and listening to the arguments of those around him—to continue. The more than 2,500 life readings he gave in the years between 1923 and his death in 1945 form some of the most engrossing and compelling "testimony" on the subject of reincarnation ever recorded.

Suddenly, then, there was a new and fantastic wealth of information—having to do with ancient religions, philosophy, universal laws, the whole history of mankind—available through the unconscious mind of Edgar Cayce. For it seemed that there was almost no question that could be put to the sleeping man that would not elicit some kind of answer. Sometimes the information confirmed and expanded knowledge of certain subjects, and sometimes it refuted it. Often, questions put to Cayce months—or even years—apart would receive the same answer, in almost identical wording.

As this new material began to pile up, more and more questions were raised in the minds of Edgar Cayce and those associated with him concerning the source of his information. Consequently, a great many readings were devoted to this subject alone.

One of the best statements in this regard was given during the course of a physical reading for a young man. After repeating the suggestion to begin the reading, Cayce opened with one of his frequent demonstrations of clairvoyance by reciting the time of day and describing the actions of the subject.

"Yes, we have the body here, John Hanson. 11:47. He has just laid aside the paper he was reading.

"In giving information concerning this body, it would be well that the body understand or have an idea of how such information may be given that there may be credence put in that which may be supplied as helpful information in the experience of this body, entity, soul, at the present.

"Then, in seeking information there are certain factors in the experience of the seeker [John Hanson] and in the channel through which such information might come [Edgar Cayce]. Desire on the part of the seeker to be shown. And, as an honest seeker, such will not be too gullible; neither will such be so encased in prejudices as to doubt that which is applicable in the experience of such seeker. Hence the information must not only be practical, but it must be rather in accord with the desires of the seeker also.

"This desire, then, is such that it must not only hold on that which is primarily the basis of all material manifestation of spiritual things, but must also have its inception in a well-balanced desire for the use of such information not only for self but for others.

"Then there may come, as for this body in the present, that which if applied may be helpful in the present experience.

"On the part of that channel [Cayce] through whom such information may come, there must be the unselfish desire to be of aid to a fellow man. Not as for self-exaltation because of being a channel. Not for self-glorification that such a channel may be well spoken of. But rather as one desirous of being a channel through which the highest spiritual forces may manifest in bringing to the material consciousness of the seeker those things that may be beneficial in a spiritual and material sense to the seeker.

"What, then, is the hypothesis of the activity that takes place during such an experience? Not merely that word telepathy, that has been coined by some untutored individuals; neither that a beneficent spirit seeking to do a service seeks out those ones and in an unseeming manner gives that from its sphere which makes for those experiences in the mind of the seeker, as some have suggested. For, if such were true at all times, there would never be a fault—if real developed spirits were in control. But rather in *this* instance is *this* the case:

"The soul of the seeker [John Hanson] is passive. The soul of the individual through whom information comes [Edgar Cayce] is positive—as the physical is subjugated into unconsciousness—and goes out on the forces that are activated by suggestion given [by the conductor of the reading] and locates the place of the seeker. And the souls commune one with another.

"Then, it is asked, what prevents the information from always being accurate, or being wholly of unquestionable nature? The fact that such information must be interpreted in material things. And that then depends upon how well the training of the physical-mental self is in such a communion."

The importance of desire on the part of the recipient was emphasized for the author by a discussion with a close relative who had received a number of Cayce readings over the years. She indicated that all her readings were personal, warm communications from the sleeping Cayce, with the exception of the very first one.

"I don't like to say this," she remarked, "but I never felt it was *my* reading. Oh, I could recognize many things in it that surely applied to my life and my way of thinking, but somehow that one reading seemed somehow remote and impersonal. And then several years ago it dawned on me what might have happened.

"You see, I was only nineteen years old at the time the reading was given. My fiance and his friend had both received life readings, and they kept urging me to have one then. I wanted to wait a few years. I never admitted to them that I just went along with the idea as a favor to them, and that secretly I resented, a bit, the pressure they had put on me. Probably I wasn't cooperating as fully as I should have been, and Cayce sensed my reluctance."

Edgar Cayce was once asked to supply a term that could be used in referring to his ability to give psychic readings, for use in some literature that was being prepared for publication. He replied, "Application of the harmonious triune; or that as may be determined by those who may 'make' a word or term to designate the various phases of the activities presented through such information.

"To be sure, it is psychic—or of the soul. As is stated, this is confusing to many whose knowledge or awareness is only of some mediumistic seance or of some activities founded upon an experience of individuals that has led to such a train of thought.

"It is the harmony of the triune—of body, mind and soul—towards the purpose of being a help, an assistance, an aid to others."

This harmonious triune was elaborated on in another Cayce reading.

"First, there is the body-physical, with all its attributes for the functioning of the body in a three-dimensional or a manifested earth plane.

"Also there is the body-mental, which is that directing influence of the physical, the mental and the spiritual emotions and manifestations of the body; or the way, the manner, in which conduct is related to self, to individuals, as well as to things, conditions and circumstances. While the mind may not be seen by the physical senses, it can be sensed by others. That is, others may sense the conclusions that have been drawn by the body-mind of an individual by the manner in which such an individual conducts himself in relationship to things, conditions or people.

"Then there is the body-spiritual, or soul-body—that eternal something that is invisible. It is only visible to that consciousness in which the individual entity in patience becomes aware of its relationships to the mental and the physical being.

"All of these, then, are one—in an entity."

Therefore, we see that, according to Cayce, the physical body is housing for the mind and the soul for purposes of existence in the earth plane.

Mind, to Cayce, is the active principle which governs man: the active force in an animate object—the spark or image of the Maker. Therefore, mind is in control of the will—that which makes one individual when we reach the earth plane. Further, said Cayce, it is mind which reasons the impressions from the senses as they manifest before the individual. Just as the psychic force is a manifestation of the soul and spirit, the mind is a manifestation of the physical.

Cayce defined the mind as being made up of many parts. First, of course, is the conscious mind, which depends upon the recognized senses of sight, hearing, smell, taste and touch to feed it material necessary for conscious reasoning.

Then there is the unconscious mind—an area in which

the Cayce readings part company, at times, with accepted scientific belief. Two broad divisions of the unconscious mind, according to Cayce, are the subconscious and the superconscious minds. The readings and science agree that the subconscious stores messages received from the conscious mind through the five senses and exerts, as well, enormous influence over the well-being of the physical body. But Cayce goes further than orthodox scientific beliefs. To Cayce, the subconscious stores full memory of all past lives which are not available to the individual's own conscious mind—although, as Cayce demonstrated in his psychic readings, these memories may be "read" by one who is able to "tune in" on them.

It is suggested by the readings that it is this part of the mind, the subconscious, that becomes, in effect, the conscious mind at the time of death of the body. You most probably will not find *this* suggestion in any psychology textbook!

Another division of the mind, according to Cayce, is the superconscious mind—another word not likely to be used by today's psychologist. It is the superconscious mind, says Cayce, which has not come into physical expression at all. *And, he continues, man's development depends upon his ability to release spiritual energy from the superconscious and bring it into conscious expression.* Mind, then, is a part of the soul.

Somewhere in the unconscious mind, too, there seems to be a mechanism which establishes contact, or attunement, between minds—as in the phenomenon of telepathy.

About the soul, Cayce once had this to say in a reading: "What, then, is a soul? What does it look like? What is its plane of experience or activity? How may ye find one?

"It may not be separated in the material world from its own place of abode in the physical body. The soul looks through the eyes of the body; it feels with the emotions; it develops awareness through the faculties in every sense —and thus adds to its body, just as food has produced a growing physical body."

Of soul memory, Cayce once said, "For know: all that the entity may know of God, or even of law or international relationships, already exists in the consciousness for the entity to be made aware of . . .

"Then, for this information to become knowledge or understanding, there must be application of self to those sources of material knowledge, yes—but with faith and trust in universal knowledge. For, as indicated by the Lawgiver, think not who will come from over the sea that a message may be brought; for, lo, it is within thine own self. For the mind and the soul are from the beginning. Thus there must come within the entity's own consciousness the awareness of how the application is to be made."

Stating the relationship between body, mind and soul, Edgar Cayce said in one reading, "When the body-physical lays aside the material body, that which, in the physical, is called the soul becomes the body of the entity; and that called the superconscious becomes the consciousness of the entity, as the subconscious is to the physical body. The subconscious becomes the mind or intellect of the body [after death]."

As an amusing example of the singleness of purpose with which Cayce's unconscious mind attuned itself to the unconscious mind of his subject, there is the case of a 23-year-old man who was given a physical reading in 1943, following his medical discharge from the service.

According to the reading, a recurrent and serious problem of amnesia had as its cause an injury to the spine, and treatment was outlined accordingly. One question submitted by this young man prior to the reading, and asked of Cayce while he was giving it was, "Can you tell me what the government records show in my trouble and what became of all my papers that were lost?"

Cayce responded immediately. "We haven't the government records; we have the body!"

The Second Source

The second major source of Cayce's information, as described by many readings, was in the collective, or universal, unconscious. According to the readings, it is in this collective unconscious that the individual unconscious has its origin.

Because of similarity of terms, we should pause here

and note the distinction between Cayce's "collective unconscious" and that defined by Carl Jung.

According to Jung, the collective unconscious is that part of the unconscious born with the individual —containing inherited patterns of instinctual behavior —that links it with all other minds in that all have a common substratum or foundation. Jung's collective unconscious is often erroneously thought of as being a group mind. "Personal unconscious" was Jung's term for that part of the mind which contains the products of individual experience.

The Cayce readings explained that every thought, every action of mankind since its beginning has been incorporated into a universal "record." Sometimes referred to in the readings as "God's Book of Remembrance," or "The Book of Life," it was most often called "the akashic records." This is the adjective form of the Sanskrit word *akasha,* and refers to the fundamental etheric substance of the universe, electro-spiritual in composition.

According to Cayce, this universal record, the akasha, is available to anyone who has developed the ability to read it. Edgar Cayce was one of many—including Socrates, Plato, Noah and Jesus—who could do this.

Cayce's ability, said the readings, had developed as a result of the experiences of many previous lives spent on earth. These included an incarnation as a high priest in pre-history Egypt, when he possessed great occult powers; as a physician and leader in Persia; as a chemist during the Trojan war; as a guard in the court of Louis XV of France; and as the British soldier, John Bainbridge, during the colonization of the United States.

One of his own life readings carries an interesting remark concerning this appearance as Bainbridge. "In the developing upon the present plane, we have much of the personality as shown in present spheres, as from that of the ability to take cognizance of detail, especially in following instructions as given from other minds or sources of information."

In the Persian incarnation, he had been wounded in desert warfare and left to die. For three days he lay on the sand, alone, without shelter, food or water. To relieve his physical suffering, he had willed consciousness to leave his body—a step in the direction of his present ability, as Edgar Cayce, to set aside his conscious mind, through trance, and make contact between his own unconscious mind and that of another individual or with the akashic records. His own readings indicated that it was this experience, coupled with the earlier experiences as a high priest in Egypt, that had begun his development as a psychic.

In a reading concerning the akashic records, Cayce was asked, "What is meant by the Book of Life?"

He replied, "That record that the individual entity writes upon the skein of time and space, through patience. [It] is opened when self has attuned to the infinite, and may be read by those attuning to that consciousness.

"The skein of time and space" appears frequently in the readings. In one reading we find, "Conditions, thoughts, activities of men in *every* clime are things; as thoughts are things. They make their impressions upon the skein of time and space. Thus, as they make for their activity, they become as records that may be read by those in accord or *attuned* to such a condition. This may be illustrated in the wave length of the radio or of such an activity. [These activities, etc.] go upon the waves of light, upon that of space. And those instruments that are *attuned* to same may hear, may experience, that which is being transmitted."

At another time, Cayce stated, "For the light moves on in time, in space; and upon that skein between them are the records written by each soul in its activity through eternity—through its awareness—not only in matter but in thought, in whatever realm the entity builds for itself in its experience, in its journey, in its activity. The physicist builds in the field of mathematics, the artist in the field of demonstration and color, the musician in sound, and so on. All are a part of the soul's ability, according to that field in which it has developed."

In another reading, he stated, "Activity of any nature, as of a voice, as of a light, produces in the natural forces a motion, which passes on, or is upon the record of time. This may be illustrated in the atomic vibrations as set in motion for those in that called the audition, the radio in its activity. Hence, light forces pass much faster; but the

38

records are upon the esoteric, or etheric, or the akashic forces, as they go along upon the wheels of time, the wings of time, or in whatever dimension we may signify as a matter of its momentum or movements. Hence, the forces that are attuned to those various incidents, periods, times, places, may be accorded to the record, the contact, as of the needle upon the record, as to how clear a rendition or audition is received, or how clear or how perfect the attunement of the instrument used, as the reproducer of same is attuned to those keepers—as may be termed—of these records. What would be indicated by the keepers? That just given; that they are the records upon the wings or the wheels of time itself."

The readings were careful to point out, however, that there is no such thing as time and space; these have been developed by man as a necessary means of measurement. "Time and space are the elements of man's own concept of the infinite, and are not realities as would be any bodily element in the earth—as a tree, a rose, a bird, an animal, or even a fellow being."

The following case seems to illustrate, quite well, Cayce's ability to read the akashic record.

In giving a life reading for a woman in May, 1939, Edgar Cayce said of one of her earlier incarnations that she had been "among those spoken of as 'holy women,' first the entity coming in contact with those activities at the death and raising of Lazarus and later with Mary, Elizabeth, Mary Magdalene, Martha. All of those were a part of the experiences of the entity, as Salome."

Seemingly, Cayce's reading was in error. Of the four Gospels, only one, St. John, incorporated the story of Lazarus, and in it there is no mention of Salome.

But more than twenty years after the reading, on December 30, 1960, the Long Island *Newsday* carried an Associated Press dispatch announcing the discovery of an ancient letter which did, indeed, place Salome at the raising of Lazarus. According to the news story, Dr. Morton Smith, associate professor of history at Columbia University, had found the letter two years earlier while studying ancient manuscripts at the Monastery of Mar Saba near Jerusalem. He had just presented it at a meeting of the Society of Biblical Literature and Exegesis, together with evidence indicating that the letter had been written by Clement of Alexandria, an author who wrote between 180 and 202 A.D., and who is generally considered to be either the creator or to have laid the foundation of Christian theology.

The letter by Clement of Alexandria contained the story of Jesus' raising Lazarus from the dead, but attributed the account to St. Mark, rather than to St. John.

It is interesting that Cayce, who read the Bible once for every year of his life, would, in trance, depart from the accepted version of the story of Lazarus. It is also most interesting that he talked of the presence of Salome at the resurrection so many years before evidence supporting this was discovered. Otherwise, we might suspect that he was receiving the information telepathically from some living person who knew of such documents.

How, then, did Edgar Cayce "know" that Salome had been present? To understand this, in line with what the readings had to say on the subject, you must consider the theory of reincarnation, together with the theory that a living person has an unconscious memory that goes back through each of his appearances on the earth plane. You must also consider it possible that Edgar Cayce could call upon this history by putting his own unconscious in tune with the unconscious of the reincarnated Salome and with the akashic records, which contain every thought and every action of mankind since its beginning.

That's quite a lot to consider; but can you think of a *better* explanation?

Other Sources?

We have now considered the two major sources of Cayce's information: the subconscious mind of his subject, and the akashic, or universal, records. Could there have been other sources as well?

The readings tell us that there may well have been others. Edgar Cayce mentioned this possibility in his talk, "What Is a Reading?" which was quoted earlier.

You will recall Cayce's statement that, although he did not operate as a "medium" in the usual sense of that word, he thought that at times he might be receiving contact from "some benevolent spirit or physician from the other side."

There were a number of readings devoted to exploring this possibility. In one of them, the question was asked, "While in the state of unconsciousness in which readings were given, could Edgar Cayce communicate with entities in the spirit plane?"

He replied, "The spirits of all that have passed from the physical plane remain about the plane until their developments carry them onward, or they are returned for their development here. When they are in the plane of communication, or remain with this sphere, any may be communicated with."

In another reading, he said, "First let it be understood that, in the material or physical plane, there is a pattern of every condition which exists in the cosmic or spiritual plane. For things spiritual and things material are but the same conditions of the same element, raised to different vibrations. For all force is *one* force.

"Remember, conditions are not changed [by death]. We find individuals, while living, at times communicative; at other times uncommunicative. There are moods . . . there are conditions under which such communications are easily attained. There are other conditions that are difficult, as it were, to meet or cope with. Just so . . . in that distant sphere."

And still another reading carried the statement, "The information as obtained and given by this body [Edgar Cayce] is gathered from the sources from which the suggestion may derive its information. In this state [self-induced hypnosis] the conscious mind becomes subjugated to the subconscious, the superconscious or soul mind, and may and does communicate with like minds, and the subconscious or soul force becomes universal. *From any subconscious mind information may be obtained either from this plane or from the impression as left by the individuals that have gone before.* [Author's italics.] As we see a mirror directly reflecting that which is before it—it is not the object itself, but that reflected. The suggestion that reaches through to the subconscious, or soul, in this state, gathers information from that as

41

reflected from what has been or is called real or material . . .

"Through the forces of the soul, through the minds of others as presented, or that have gone on before; through the subjugation of the physical forces in this manner, the body [Edgar Cayce] obtains the information."

In this same reading, given in 1923, Edgar Cayce was asked if the thoughts of one person could affect another person, either mentally or physically. The sleeping man answered, "Depending upon the development of the person to whom the thought may be directed. The possibilities of developing thought transference are first being shown—evolution, you see. The individuals of this plane are developing and will develop this as the senses are developed."

Cayce was once asked to describe how thought transference or telepathy might be accomplished, or learned. His answer was simple. "First, begin between selves. Set a definite time and each at that moment put down what the other is doing. Do this twenty days. And ye shall find ye have the key to telepathy."

Normally, in the trance state, Cayce did not receive his information via a "control," such as Arthur Ford's "Fletcher." And yet an extraordinary occurrence, on October 9, 1933, seems to indicate that at times a discarnate entity may have spoken through him.

The first paragraph of the waking suggestion had been given to Cayce following a reading concerning his own psychic work. Suddenly he announced, "Some good information here!"

Gertrude Cayce, who was conducting the reading, said, "May we have it at this time?"

For the next ten minutes, Cayce spoke on the subject of the personality of discarnate entities and their influence on our thinking—particularly in connection with great movements in political, economic, social or religious thought. This included the statement, "So we begin to see how the thought, or mental movement that produces thought in the minds of souls in the earth may be influenced by that movement outside of self."

The topic of the reading was interesting, if difficult to comprehend because of the intricate wording. Most in-

42

teresting, though, is the fact that it was delivered by Cayce in a distinctly British voice, unlike any accent he had ever used before or would use again in a reading! The secretary reported, "It sounded like Edgar Cayce, but more as if he were acting the part of an Englishman—trying to repeat the tone of voice and comments of an Englishman standing by; not at all as if the Englishman had taken over."

In 1934, at the end of a routine physical reading, Cayce was given the suggestion to wake up. Instead of doing so, he began to speak. "There are some here that would speak with those that are present, if they desire to so communicate with them."

There were four people in the room in addition to Cayce: his wife, Gertrude; his secretary, Gladys Davis; Mildred Davis; and Cayce's father, Leslie B. Cayce.

Gertrude Cayce said, "We desire to have at this time that which would be given."

After a long pause, Edgar Cayce began a strange monologue. "Don't all speak at once!" Then another pause. "Yes, I knew you would be waiting." There followed a one-sided conversation which included such comments as, "All together now, huh? Uncle Porter too? He was able to ease it right away, huh? Who? Dr. House. No. Oh, no—no, she is all right. Yes, lots better. . . . Tell Tommy what? Yes! Lynn? Yes, he's at home . . . Oh, you knew that! . . . Well, how about the weather? Oh, the weather doesn't affect you now—doesn't change—Oh, you have what you want . . . depends on where you go. . . . For Gertrude? Yes, she is here . . . she hears you. Oh, yes."

Mrs. Cayce didn't hear anyone but Edgar Cayce, and said so.

Edgar Cayce continued. "Sure, she hears you; don't you hear her talking?"

Again Gertrude Cayce asked for the message. This time she received some interpretation of what Cayce had been discussing. It included an explanation that ". . . Mama and Dr. House and Uncle Porter and the baby [possibly the child born to Edgar and Gertrude Cayce some years before, who lived only a few weeks] . . . we are all here. . . . We have reached, together, that place where we see the light and know the pathway to the Savior is along the narrow way that leads to His Throne. We are on that plane where you have heard it said that the body and the mind are one with those things we have built. . . . Well, we will be waiting for you!"

Naturally, there was much interest in the source and meaning of this message, and so a reading was given on July 17, 1934, for the purpose of finding out more about it. In part, the reading went as follows.

The suggestion was given, "You will have before you the body and inquiring mind of Edgar Cayce and all present in this room, in regard to the experience following the reading Monday afternoon, July 9, 1934, explaining to us what happened . . . and why at that particular time, answering the questions that may be asked."

Cayce said, "Yes, we have the body, and the inquiring mind, Edgar Cayce, and those present in the room July 9, 1934.

"In giving that which may be helpful, for the moment turn to that known as the body of self and by those present in the room respecting what is ordinarily termed spirit communication or . . . should be (and that which has caused much of the dissension) . . . *soul* communication. For the soul lives on and is released from a house of clay. The activities in the world of matter are only changed in their relationships to that which produces them and that which the physical body sees in material or three-dimensional form.

"There were those that were in attune . . . through the vibrations from that sounded in the room at that particular period . . . and these sought (many—even many that spoke not) to communicate that there might be known not only their continued existence in a world of matter but of finer matter. They sought, through those channels through which the soul-force of the body was passing at the particular time, to produce that which would make their presence known.

"Although the various communications given at the time were from those thought to be dead (from the physical viewpoint) or in other realms, yet their souls, their personalities, their individualities live on. The personalities are lost gradually . . . [as they develop in the other plane]."

44

Cayce was asked, "Why did we hear only one side of the conversation?"

"Denseness of matter to the spirit realm," he replied. "All who attuned themselves *felt* the presence of those influences. The Master said, 'They that have ears to hear, let them hear.' There be none so deaf as those who do not *want* to hear. All could hear if they would attune themselves to the realm of the activity during such an experience. The conversation dealt with matters that were to them, are to them, very vital in their experiences in the present plane.

"How, some would ask, did the body, Edgar Cayce, or soul, attune self at that particular period and yet not remember in the physical consciousness? This is because *the soul passes from the body* into those realms where information may be obtained. Help was sought on the ninth of July for the physical condition of a body [referring to the physical reading given just before Cayce began to "converse" with several departed relatives]. This realm from which such information is obtainable is either from those that have passed into the realm of subconscious activity or from the subconscious and superconscious activity of the one through whom information is being sought. This particular body, Edgar Cayce, was able to attune self to the varied realms of activity by laying aside the physical consciousness. If the body, from its material and mental development, were to be wholly conscious of that through which it passes in its soul's activity in such realms, the strain would be too great. Material activity could be unbalanced and the body become demented. And he is thought crazy enough anyway!"

Humor was ever-present in the Cayce readings. This last comment undoubtedly alluded to the many people who were unable to accept the validity of clairvoyance—even when it was demonstrated by Edgar Cayce so well, and for so many years—and thought of him as "some kind of a nut."

A Visit From an Old Friend

Edgar Cayce experienced visions throughout his lifetime. Often they were symbolic in nature, and special readings were given to gain interpretation of them.

45

One such vision occurred on October 22, 1933. This is the way Edgar Cayce described it in a report given in 1936.

"Some years ago I had a very warm personal friend who was an executive of the Western Union Telegraph Company in Chicago. We met quite often, and in our discussions of various subjects the question frequently arose between us as to whether or not there was a survival of personality. It usually ended jokingly with one of us saying, 'Well, whichever one goes first will communicate with the other.'

"During the last few years of my friend's life, we did not meet, but we corresponded intermittently. Then I was notified of his death in April, 1933.

"Several months afterwards I was sitting alone in my living room, listening to the radio. The program was Seth Parker's. Members of the group had decided they would sing songs which their loved ones had been fond of during their lifetime. One lady asked that they sing, 'Sweet Hour of Prayer.' Another asked her which one of her husbands had liked that song. I remember that I was very much amused, and leaned back in my chair, smiling to myself.

"Suddenly I felt as if there was a presence in the room. I was cold, and felt something uncanny or unusual taking place. The program was still on.

"When I looked toward the radio, I realized that my friend, who had died several months before, was sitting in front of the radio listening to the program. He turned and smiled at me, saying, 'Cayce, there IS the survival of personality. I KNOW! And a life of service and prayer is the only one to live.'

"I was shaking all over. He said nothing more, and just seemed to disappear.

"The program finished, I turned off the radio. It still appeared as if the room was full of some presence. As I switched off the light and climbed the stairs, I could hear many voices coming from the darkened room.

"Jumping in bed and shivering from cold, I aroused my wife. She asked me why I hadn't turned off the radio. I assured her that I had. She opened the door, and said, 'I hear it—I hear voices.' We both did.

"What was it?"

CHAPTER FOUR

OUT OF BODY

The following is an excerpt from a talk given by Edgar Cayce in August, 1931.

"Let me tell you of an experience of my own. I feel that it was a very real experience, and as near an illustration of what happens at death as it would be possible to put into words. On going into the unconscious state one time to obtain information for an individual, I recognized that I was leaving my body. There was just a direct, straight, and narrow line in front of me, like a shaft of white light. On either side was fog and smoke, and many shadowy figures who seemed to be crying to me for help, and begging me to come aside to the state they occupied.

"As I followed along the shaft of light, the way began to clear. The figures on either side grew more distinct; they took on clearer form. But there was a continual beckoning back, or the attempt to sidetrack me and bring me aside from my purpose. Yet with the narrow way in front of me I kept going straight ahead. After a bit I passed to where the figures were merely shadows attempting to assist; they urged me on rather than attempted to stop me. Then they took on more form, and they seemed to be occupied with their own activities. When they paid any attention to me at all it was rather to urge me on.

"Finally I came to a hill, where there was a mount and a temple. I entered this temple and found in it a very large room, very much like a library. They were the books of people's lives, for each person's activities were a matter of actual record, it seemed, and I merely had to pull down a record of the individual for whom I was seeking information.

"I have to say as Paul did, 'Whether I was in the spirit or out of the spirit, I cannot tell.' "

This experience indicates, we think, the delicate balance of Edgar Cayce's being while he was in trance. Many readings confirm this and serve, as well, to amplify our understanding of the condition known as "out of body."

In this state, Cayce's body remained on the couch with the unconscious mind in control. Suspended above him, at a height of about eighteen inches, lay the conscious mind which had been temporarily set aside.

The readings explained that in this state, Cayce operated much in the manner of a radio receiver, tuned to the proper channel for receiving the information sought in the reading. Any interference—such as the asking of irrelevant questions, antagonistic thoughts on the part of anyone connected with getting the reading, and so on—could disrupt the process by creating a sort of psychic static.

Any physical interference with Cayce's body, or with his conscious mind, or "personality," suspended above it, could have alarming consequences. Once, during a public session, someone who didn't understand this out of body state passed a sheet of paper to Hugh Lynn Cayce across the form of his sleeping father. Cayce immediately stopped talking, and went into a cataleptic silence which lasted for several hours. This had never happened before, and no one knew what to do about it. When Cayce *did* wake up, he did so with alarming speed—jackknifing himself to a standing position at the foot of the couch.

Needless to say, precautions were taken to see that this sort of thing never happened again!

In a reading given April 30, 1934, the question was asked, "What has caused the jerking and twitching movement of Edgar Cayce's physical body during readings given within the last few months?

His answer serves to further our understanding of out-of-body experiences. "Not perfect accord in the physical body of Edgar Cayce, partially," he said. "Not perfect accord in the minds of those present as to the purpose of seeking in each instance.

"For, where lack of harmony prevails and a soul enters into the veil where there may be the realm of those influences that become so impelling in their activity in material things, *what* a strain! The wonder may ever be that there isn't and has not been much greater contortion, save that—as given—the body-mind, the body-consciousness, the soul-consciousness has been attuned to much that to many would have been a breaking point.

"Not that the body is to be pampered, nor to be shown other than that deference which each individual present does hold. But know, all that draw near, what they are dealing with: that the soul is very *near* at all times to *being away from* the body, seeking. Hence the care, the caution, that should be taken by those that feel they have any interest in the body, life, or in the *greater* life of the entity in its seeking and its desire to serve."

As one further illustration of this, there was the morning on which apparently a few too many questions were asked of the sleeping Cayce. Showing some irritation, he abruptly ended the reading by saying, "We are through."

And then an extraordinary thing happened. As Cayce was being given the normal suggestion to awaken, his body nearly turned a somersault. His head bent over to almost touch his feet, and he stayed in that strange position until the waking suggestion was completed. He awoke normally, then, and remarked that he felt "exuberant—*fine!*"

Later that day, another reading was given on the subject of the Cayce work. He was asked to explain why he had demonstrated such a strange physical reaction at the close of the morning's reading.

He answered, "As was seen, through the seeking of irrelevant questions there was antagonism manifested. This made for a contraction of those channels through which the activity of the psychic forces operates in the material body. . . . The natural reactions are for sudden contraction when changing suddenly from the mental-spiritual to material [from the hypnotic to the conscious state].

"For, as evidenced by that which has been given, there is the touching—with the mental beings of those present in the room or at such manifestations—of the most delicate mechanism that may be imagined."

Levels of Consciousness

Apparently, in seeking certain information about an individual or an event, Cayce's unconscious mind operated on many levels, or in various dimensions.

There are many indications, in the readings, of his "seeing" certain activities at the various levels on his way to the eventual source of much of his information: an old man who handed him a large book containing the data he wanted. He described, for example, what appeared to be classrooms in which teachers were preparing souls for their next return to earth.

Many readings point to the existence of various planes within what Cayce called his "sphere of communication," peopled by entities on the various planes according to their levels of development in the long, hard struggle toward ultimate perfection. Mental attunement with any of these entities was possible.

One reading stated, "Each and every soul entity, or earthly entity passing through the earth's plane, leaves in that plane those conditions that are impressions from the soul or spiritual entity of the individual. This, then, becomes the fact, the real fact, in the material world.

"The body, Edgar Cayce, in the psychic or subconscious condition, is able to reach all subconscious minds, when directed to such by suggestion—whether in the material world or in the spiritual world, provided the spiritual entity has not passed entirely into another level. Then we reach only those radiations left in the earth's plane. These are taken on again when re-entering the earth's plane, whether the entity is conscious of the same or not. The consciousness of this movement and development must eventually be reached by all."

This is the way Edgar Cayce once recalled the experience of getting his information:

"I see myself as a tiny dot out of my physical body, which lies inert before me. I find myself oppressed by darkness and there is a feeling of terrific loneliness. Suddenly, I am conscious of a beam of white light. I move upward in the light, knowing that I must follow it or be lost.

"As I move along this path of light, I gradually become conscious of various levels upon which there is movement. Upon the first levels there are vague, horrible shapes, grotesque forms such as one sees in nightmares. Passing on, there begin to appear on either side misshapen forms of human beings with some part of the body magnified. Again there is change and I become conscious of gray-hooded forms moving downward. Gradually, these become lighter in color. Then the direction changes and these forms move upward and the color of the robes grows rapidly lighter.

"Next, there begin to appear on either side vague outlines of houses, walls, trees, etc., but everything is motionless. As I pass on, there is more light and movement in what appear to be normal cities and towns. With the growth of movement I become conscious of sounds, at first indistinct rumblings, then music, laughter, and singing of birds. There is more and more light, the colors become very beautiful, and there is only a blending of sound and color. Quite suddenly, I come upon a hall of records. It is a hall without walls, without a ceiling, but I am conscious of seeing an old man who hands me a large book, a record of the individual for whom I seek information."

Keeper of the Records

"My! What a large volume!" said Cayce at the beginning of a reading for a seven-year-old girl in 1936.

"The cleanest record I've ever experienced. The book is the cleanest. And yet I had never thought of any of them not being perfectly clean before." Thus Cayce ended a reading, also in 1936, for a three-year-old boy.

What did Cayce mean by "record," by "book?" Why, at the beginning of each life reading, did Cayce seem to be thumbing back through some sort of soul diary—not only to the birth date of the person for whom the reading was being given, but further, still, back into the history of previous lives spent on the earth by the individual? For it was always the same in a Cayce life reading: he put himself into trance and then "took himself" to the "old man with the books." There he got his information.

In a reading given in September, 1933, Cayce explained this. "To bring from one realm to another those experiences through which an entity, a soul, may pass in obtaining those reflections that are necessary for transmission of the information sought, it becomes necessary (for the understanding of those in that realm seeking) to have that which is to the mental being put in the language of that being, as near as it is possible to do justice to the subject."

Cayce, then, was using symbology when he referred to "books." Now he explained why. "[The information is given] in the form of pictures or expressions, that there may be the conveying to the mind of the seeker something in his own type of experience, as to how the transmission of the activity takes place. Of what forces? The psychic or soul forces, that are akin to what? The Creative Forces, or that called God.

"So the body [of Edgar Cayce] arrives at a place in which there is kept the records of all; as signified in speaking of the Book of Life, or to indicate or symbolize that each entity, each soul in its growth, may find its way back to the Creative Influences that are promised in and through Him that gives—and is—Life; and finds this as a separate, a definite, an integral part of the very soul."

Thus Cayce explained that each soul, in each experience of assuming bodily form, makes a record. It gains in development; it loses. It exercises its free will, given by God, for good or for evil in each earthly appearance. ". . . Hence, symbolized as being in books; and the man the keeper, as the keeper of the records . . .

"So, in the materializations for the concept of those that seek to know, to be enlightened; to the world, long has there been sought that as in books. To many the question naturally arises, then: are there literally books? To a mind that thinks books, literally *books!* As it would be for the mind that in its passage from the material plane into rest would require Elysian fields with birds, with flowers; it must find the materialized form of that portion of the Maker in that realm wherein that entity, that soul, would enjoy such in *that* sphere of activity. As houses built in wood. Wood, in its essence, as given, is what? Books, in their essence, are what? What is the more real, the book with its printed pages, its gilt edges, or the essence of that told of in the book? Which is the more real, the love manifested in the Son, the Savior, for His brethren, or the essence of love that may be seen even in the vilest of passion? They are one."

CHAPTER FIVE

EDGAR CAYCE'S DEVELOPMENT AS A PSYCHIC

As we have mentioned, it was not until 1923 that the subject of reincarnation entered the Cayce readings. And yet there is a hint of things to come in a reading given the day after Cayce's forty-second birthday, on March 19, 1919. It is one of the most fascinating readings in the Cayce files, in terms of the clear and concise way it explains his psychic work.

Background for the reading was furnished by Cayce as follows: "In December, 1918, I received a request from a Mr. Thrash, who was editor of a newspaper in Cleburne, Texas, for a physical reading. He also wanted to ask some questions about business. Among these letters was one in which he asked for my birthdate; he said he wanted to have my horoscope cast. Soon after this I received several communications from astrologers telling me that on March 19, 1919, I would be able to give a reading that would be of more interest to mankind as a whole than any I would be able to give during that year. I was asked to make this reading public. I did not care for notoriety, which I felt this would give, yet I was curious and desired to know what the reading would give at this time. I attempted it—and the following reading is the result. The questions asked in this reading were prepared by myself." ·

Reading: March 19, 1919

Conductor: You will have before you the body and the inquiring mind of Edgar Cayce, and you will tell us how the psychic work is accomplished through this body and will answer any other questions that I will ask you respecting this work.

Cayce: We have the body, Edgar Cayce. We have had it before. In this state the conscious mind is under subjugation of the subconscious or soul mind. The information obtained and given by this body is obtained through the power of mind over mind, or power of mind over physical matter, or obtained by the suggestion as given to the active part of the subconscious mind. It obtains its information from that which it has gathered, either from other subconscious minds—put in touch with the power of the suggestion of the mind controlling the speaking faculties of this body—or from minds that have passed into the Beyond, which leave their impressions and are brought in touch by the power of the suggestion.

What is known to one subconscious mind or soul is known to another, whether conscious of the fact or not. The subjugation of the conscious mind putting the subconscious mind in action in this manner or in one of the other of the manners as directed, this body obtains its information when in the subconscious state.

Conductor: Is this information always correct?

Cayce: Correct in so far as the suggestion is in the proper channel or in accord with the action of subconscious or soul matter.

Conductor: Do the planets have anything to do with the ruling of the destiny of men? If so, what? And what do they have to do with this body?

Cayce: They do. In the beginning, as our own planet, Earth, was set in motion, the placing of other planets began the ruling of the destiny of all matter as created, just as the division of waters was and is ruled by the moon in its path about the Earth; just so as in the higher creation, as it began, is ruled by the action of the planets about the Earth.

The strongest power in the destiny of man is the sun, first; then the closer planets, or those that are coming in ascendency at the time of the birth of the individual. But let it be understood here, no action of any planet or any of the phases of the sun, moon, or any of the heavenly bodies surpass the rule of man's individual will power—the power given by the Creator of man in the beginning, when he became a living soul, with the power of choosing for himself.

The inclination of man is ruled by the planets under which he is born; for the destiny of man lies within the sphere or scope of the planets. With the given position of the solar system at the time of the birth of an individual, it can be worked out—that is, the inclinations and actions without the will power taken into consideration.

As in this body [Edgar Cayce] born March 18, 1877, three minutes past three o'clock, with the sun descending, on the wane, the moon in the opposite side of the earth (old moon), Uranus at its zenith, hence the body is ultra in its actions. Neptune closest in conjunction, or Neptune as it is termed in astrological survey, in the ninth house; Jupiter, the higher force of all the planets, save the sun, in descendency, Venus just coming to horizon, Mars just set, Saturn—to whom all insufficient matter is cast at its decay—opposite the face of the moon. Hence the inclination as the body is controlled by the astrological survey at the time of the birth of this body, either (no middle ground for this body) very good or very bad, very religious or very wicked, very rich or always losing, very much in love or hate, very much given to good works or always doing wrong, governed entirely by the will of the body. Will is the educational factor of the body; thence the patience, the persistence, the ever-faithful attention that should be given to the child when it is young.

As to the forces of this body, the psychical is obtained through the action of Uranus and of Neptune. Always it has been to this body and always will, just outside the action of firearms, yet ever within them, just saved financially and spiritually by the action of great amounts of water. The body should live close to the sea, should always have done so. The body is strange to other bodies in all of its actions, in the psychical life, in all of its ideas as expressed in the spiritual life as to its position on all matters pertaining to political, religious or economical positions. This body will either be very rich or very poor.

Conductor: Will this work hurt the body?

Cayce: Only through the action of power of suggestion over the body. This body is controlled in its work through the psychical or the mystic or spiritual. It is governed by the life that is led by the person who is guiding the subconscious when in this state, or by the line of thought that is given to create ideas of expression to the subconscious.

As the ideas given the subconscious to obtain its information are good, the body becomes better; if bad or wicked, it becomes under the same control. Then the body should not be held responsible save through the body controlling the body at such times.

Conductor: Can this power be used to be of assistance to humanity and also to obtain financial gain?

Cayce: There are many channels through which information obtained from this body in this state would be of assistance to humanity. To obtain financial gain from these is to obtain that which is just and right to those dependent upon this body for the things of life. Not those that would be destructive to the bodies themselves, physically or mentally, but that which is theirs by right should be obtained for such information.

As to which is the best channel, it depends as to whether the information desired is in accord with the ideas of the body from which they are attempting to obtain them.

When credence is given to the work in a material way, anyone is willing to pay in a financial way for such information; but without credence there can be nothing obtained.

Conductor: Is there any other information that this body should have now?

Cayce: The body should keep close in touch with the spiritual side of life—with sincerity to the spiritual side of life—if he is to be successful mentally, physically, psychically and financially.

The safest brace is the spiritual nature of the body; sincerity of the work done or obtained through any channel with which this body is connected is governed by the masses through the action of the body towards the spiritual.

*   *   *

We call particular attention to the statement in this reading, "The body . . . is governed by the life that is led by the person who is guiding the subconscious when in this state, or by the line of thought that is given to create ideas of expression to the subconscious."

In giving this reading, at the specific request of a man interested in astrology, Cayce had referred to the role of the planets in determining the destiny of man. Cayce's own psychic abilities were explained in the light of planetary influences, with no mention of past lives. Perhaps this was because Mr. Thrash had no apparent interest in, or knowledge of, theories concerning reincarnation. Or perhaps it was simply because Cayce himself, and those around him, were not yet ready to accept this new expansion in the scope of information received through Cayce's unconscious mind. None of the information given in this reading was later refuted by other readings. It simply went so far and no farther.

But in 1923 a man named Arthur Lammers, a wealthy printer of Dayton, Ohio, heard of Edgar Cayce and made a special trip to Selma, Alabama, to visit him and watch him work. He persuaded Cayce to return with him to Dayton for a special series of readings, since he was unable to remain in Selma long enough to get the answers to some of his questions.

Lammers' intention was to try to obtain, through the readings, information concerning matters of universal significance. Why was a man born? What was his reason for living? What happened to him when he died? He was impressed by the accuracy with which Cayce could "see" within the human body, tell what was wrong with it and how to repair it. But Lammers sensed that there were areas of knowledge available to Cayce that so far had not been touched. An intelligent, well-educated man, Lammers had long been a student of astrology, theology and

57

philosophy. Here, possibly, were answers to questions that had puzzled him for years.

So it was into a new climate of interest that Cayce's remarkable statement, at the end of a reading given for Lammers, was made: "He was once a monk." With these five simple words, Cayce opened the door to an entirely new aspect in his work. The reading had been set up for the purpose of casting a horoscope for Lammers. Cayce had volunteered this new and startling information at the end of an otherwise unremarkable reading.

A series of readings followed, so positive in their statements concerning the *reality* of reincarnation, that Lammers now persuaded Cayce to move his family to Dayton. He paid their train fares and furnished housing to enable them to do this.

Soon after the move to Dayton, Cayce discussed, in one reading, the influence of the planets on the destinies of individuals. This portion of the reading, given four years after the one quoted earlier in this chapter, matched the earlier one almost word for word. Cayce said, "Just as the division of waters was ruled and is ruled by the moon in its path about the Earth, just so is the higher creation . . . ruled by its action in conjunction with the planets about the Earth. The strongest force used in the destiny of man is the sun first, then the closer planets to the Earth, or those that are coming to ascension at the time of the birth of the individual . . .

"The inclinations of man are ruled by the planets under which he is born, for the destiny of man lies within the sphere or scope of the planets . . .

"But let it be understood here, no action of any planet or the phases of the sun, moon or any of the heavenly bodies surpasses the rule of man's WILL POWER!—the power given by the Creator of man in the beginning, when he became a living soul with the power of choosing for himself."

Cayce contrasted horoscopes and life readings in the following reading given at the request of Arthur Lammers:

Conductor: You will have before you the psychic work as done by Edgar Cayce. You will answer the following questions as I ask them regarding this work.

Cayce: Yes, we have this work here, with all of its modifications, and the various channels through which it may manifest in the various phenomena of the psychic forces. Ready for questions.

Conductor: Is this body when in this state able to give a horoscope reading?

Cayce: Able. But would not be worth very much to anyone.

Conductor: What is a horoscope reading?

Cayce: That in which the planets and their relative forces having to do with the planets that control the actions without respect of will, or without respect of the earthly existences through which the body has passed.

Conductor: Do horoscope readings include former appearances in the earth plane?

Cayce: Not at all. The former appearances and the relation of the solar forces in the universe have their relations to what might be termed life readings, or experiences. For, as has been shown and given, horoscope, the science of the solar system and its relation to various phases of earth's existence, may mean for anyone.

In life existence in earth's plane and the entity's relation to other spheres, there is a different condition. For the sojourn in other spheres than earth's plane controls more the conditions or the *urge* of the individual. Just as we see in the earth plane an individual is controlled by the surroundings, or by the circumstances that have to do with the individual, yet we find the urge, the latent forces, that would give an individual, or two groups, or two individuals raised under the same environment, of the same blood, different urges. These are received from experiences the spirit entity gains in other spheres, correlated with its present circumstance and condition.

These should never be confused. For, to gain a horoscope is only the mathematical calculation of earth's position in the universe at any given time, while in the life reading would be the correlation of the individual with a given time and place, with its relative force as applied and received through other spheres and manifested in earth's sphere in other flesh, and the development being the extenuation of the soul's development manifested in the earth plane through subconscious forces of a body or entity.

Conductor: Give the words that should be given to this body to obtain a reading of this kind, a life reading, with the former appearances and their effect in the present life on an individual.

Cayce: "You will have before you the body— (giving name and place of the individual at birth, the name at birth as given) and you will give the relation of this entity and the universe, and the universal forces, giving the conditions that are as personalities latent, and exhibited, in the present life. Also the former appearances in the earth's plane, giving time, place, name and that in that life which built or retarded the development for the entity, giving the abilities of the present entity and that to which it may attain, and how."

In this, you see, we will find the effect not only of the present environment, as it has been, as it may be, but the effect of the past experiences and through what sphere these were obtained.

We are through for the present.

* * *

Compare this information with that given in the 1919

reading, and you can see the ever-broadening scope of Cayce's information.

But it wasn't just the information that was expanding; Cayce's ability to receive it was expanding as well. Just as the experiences of his earlier incarnations, according to the readings, had prepared him for the work he was able to do in *this* lifetime, so the ability itself developed during the forty-three years it was utilized.

An example of this is shown in a reading given in November, 1932, in which Cayce was asked to explain a conscious vision he had experienced while engaged in teaching a Sunday school class. In the vision, he had seen a number of people of the Jewish faith enter the church and stand about, listening to Cayce's words.

Said the reading, "As should be understood by the body, this was an experience, real, literal, in the sense that we as individuals are ever encompassed about by those that are drawn to us by the vibration or attitude concerning conditions that are existent in the experience of entities or souls seeking their way to their Maker." Explaining this further, the reading told Cayce that, since the subject of his lesson had been certain activities of the Jews, "so there was gathered mostly those that had held in common a faith and desire in this particular phase of experience. The carnal eye was then lifted for Cayce, so that he saw; even as the servant of Elisha saw those that camped between those that would hinder Elisha in his service to his people.

"*As the visions as a child, then, Cayce is again entering that phase of development or experience where there may be in the physical consciousness periods when there may be visioned those that are seeking in the spirit realm for that which will aid them to understand their relations with the Whole.* [Author's italics.]

"As has been given to this body Cayce, to this peculiar people has he been sent; as one—one—that may aid many to come to a better understanding of their relationships to the Creator and their relationships to their fellow man . . .

"Know that the body is being given more and more the opportunity to minister to not only those in the material things in the material life, but these as seen who are seeking in the Borderland, those that are to many a loved one in the spirit land they are seeking—seeking."

So, according to the reading, Cayce was now to serve as a help to those in the spirit world, as well as to those on earth! Can you imagine the responsibility he must have felt when this information was given to him?

The reading carried a warning to Cayce. "Do not become self-important, nor self-exalting. Be rather selfless, that there may come to all who come under the sound of thy voice, to all that come in thy presence, as they look upon thine countenance, the knowledge and feeling that, indeed, this man has been in the presence of his Maker; he has seen the visions of those expanses we all seek—to pull the veil aside that we may peer into the future. As ye may become a teacher to those that are 'beyond the veil' also, how glorious must be thy words even then to those that falter in their steps day by day!"

In June, 1936, a reading asked, "Is there any special preparation necessary for [Cayce] to make, consciously, for his psychic work as it will develop within the next few years?"

The sleeping Cayce answered, "There are many experiences that remain as those promises that are a portion of the entity's development in this material plane. These are the stepping-stones, the milestones along the path of efficiency or of the abilities in the experience of the entity to become more and more *efficient*—as would be termed.

"But as for preparation, is a sound apple prepared at once or does it *grow* that way? Is the sun's light all of a glow or has it *grown* that way? The consciousness of the ability to serve is only by service, not by just wishing. But how has it been given? Desire of such a nature as to act, as to will, and act with the fusion of will and desire towards that purpose! *Fear* being cast aside by the very abilities of the self-submerging of the physical consciousness through those influences as has so oft been indicated, makes for an attunement to those sources sought by the individual seeker.

"The preparations, the *desire* ever, the will to do, are ever present. Then the variations are only according to that purpose for which and through which the seeker is making the attunement for self.

"As to those influences for greater preservation, greater abilities; as those promises have come, and there are the fulfillments in the experience to that voice from within and that meeting constantly within the temples of the physical forces where there has been the consecrating of self for service, there comes that growth that may be more and more helpful. But keep the faith!"

This particular reading, by the way, indicated that Edgar Cayce was doing a fine job of working out his karma. By being of service to his fellow man, through his chosen work, he was making great progress in atoning for the weaknesses of the flesh of some of his earlier lives.

"The abilities of this entity, then, arise from those experiences [in past incarnations] when the ego, the self, was submerged in a service for the fellow man. The *confusion* [disturbances in Cayce's present life caused by some tendency toward being too critical of others, as well as a terrible temper which bothered him throughout his lifetime] arises from those experiences when self-indulgence, self-aggrandizement, made for the purposes as with desire and will in its association with circumstance or conditions in the experience of the entity."

As so often happened in readings, this one gave Cayce some advice toward controlling his temper, with the statement, "Easy is the way of those that would find fault; greater is the sounding of the cymbal than the coo of the dove. Or as has been manifested in those of old, indeed in the storm, in the thunder, in the lightning is the *power* shown, but the activity is rather in the still, small voice that speaks from within." And again came the warning against letting anyone use Cayce's abilities for selfish purposes: "Oft there is confusion in the minds of those that may seek or may study, in that there is the lack of understanding that *psychic is of the soul*; whether of groups or whether of individuals that manifest in any given experience."

Such advice was important to Cayce, for his psychic abilities were always dependent upon his mental and physical health. There were times, throughout his life, when he would put himself into hypnotic sleep but no reading would come. Often the problem stemmed from worry; and worry, in turn, usually stemmed from finances.

For the giving of psychic readings—particularly during the dark years of the depression—was far from a lucrative occupation. Any emotional disturbance could affect his ability to do his work, as could any physical ailment. Usually, however, the reading would be obtained at a later time.

Occasionally—especially during the early years of Cayce's career—unscrupulous people would try to take advantage of his abilities, to use them in money-making ventures. Even if they gained by it, Cayce always lost. Whenever this sort of thing happened, he suffered afterwards from severe headaches or other physical problems. In surrendering his conscious mind to his unconscious mind, he was completely at the mercy of those attending him. It was for this reason that the readings were generally conducted by Cayce's father, by his wife, or by his son. Even with these precautions, it required much courage to do the work he did.

CHAPTER SIX

UNUSUAL CLAIRVOYANCE

It has been estimated that during his lifetime Edgar Cayce spoke in some two dozen different languages while giving readings, although he had conscious knowledge only of English. Here are two examples.

Cayce was living in Selma, Alabama in 1917 when a woman in Palermo, Sicily, heard of him and wrote to request proper diagnosis and treatment for an abdominal illness. Her letter was in Italian, so Cayce sent it off to a friend in Tuscaloosa for translation.

The reading, when it was given in January 27, 1918, was entirely in Italian. An Italian fruit dealer, hastily summoned to Cayce's studio from his stand nearby, was able to take it down in longhand and dictate the translation to the stenographer afterwards.

And here's another case. On July 11, 1933, Edgar Cayce began to give a life reading for Hans Mueller of New York, who had been born 53 years earlier in Frankfort, Germany.

The customary reading suggestion was made. Cayce repeated it to himself and then began his usual custom of going back over the dates from the present until he reached the subject's date of birth. Then he said, "Yes, we have the entity and those relations with the universe and universal forces, that are latent and manifested in the personality of the present entity, known as Hans Mueller."

Now, however, he became silent. After a long pause, he began to utter a series of German words. Cayce, as we've mentioned, had no knowledge of the German language; nor did his wife, who was conducting the reading; nor did his secretary, Gladys Davis (Turner), who could only take down the words phonetically. (Mr. Mueller later translated these to a group of exclamations, including, "Little corner place! Little one! Little child! I make one speech; I speak German! Oh, my, I speak German! Oh, my, no!" Mueller thought that some of the expressions, such as "little one" and "little child" might have been words used by his grandparents to express their delight at his birth. This seems plausible when we consider that Cayce always seemed to take himself back in time and be psychically "present" at the events and places he described in his life readings.)

After completing the series of German expressions, Cayce said abruptly, "We are through."

The reading was attempted again the next day. Cayce had no trouble getting it, for it was wholly in English.

In September of that year, a day was set aside for readings in which special questions about Cayce's work could be answered. During the morning session, Cayce was asked to explain why Hans Mueller's reading had been disrupted so strangely.

There was no hesitation on Cayce's part; his unconscious memory, functioning perfectly as always, immediately recalled the event. He explained that the one who had been attempting to guide him in obtaining the information spoke only German. As soon as it was clear that no one in the room could understand the language, the communication was cut off.

Then he was asked, "What is the interpretation of the German words given?"

Cayce's answer carried some rebuke. "This is simply curiosity," he said. "Learn German!"

One of the most remarkable examples of Cayce's clairvoyance can be found in a reading given on October 9, 1933. Four questions and answers, appearing in the readings exactly in the order in which they appear below, illustrate how rapidly and clearly Cayce's unconscious mind could analyze objects brought to his attention.

The first question concerned a dark brown liquid used for treating various gum disorders. It was recommended so often in the readings that eventually it was produced under the brand name "Ipsab."

Conductor: I hold in my hand a bottle of Ipsab recently prepared according to a formula given through this channel. Is this correctly prepared, and will it in this form do what is expected of it?

Cayce: It will.

66

Conductor: It is correctly prepared, then?

Cayce: Good.

Conductor: Would you suggest any changes which would benefit it?

Cayce: Deeper clarification only, or clearer of contamination of the water used, where there's not so much matter that has made—or does make—for a concentration of same.

By way of the next question, Cayce turned from being a sleeping "druggist" to a sleeping "editor." Some pamphlets based on the readings had just been completed, and the writer wanted to know if they accurately represented the material.

Conductor: "I hold in my hand copies of two papers, *Oneness of All Force* and *Meditation*———"

Cayce: (interrupting) "They are very good, both of 'em. Use them as they are! Very good looking papers!"

CHAPTER SEVEN

AURAS

"Auras" is the name of the last A.R.E. booklet authored by Edgar Cayce. Written in collaboration with his biographer and friend, Thomas Sugrue, and published just after Cayce's death in January, 1945, it begins:

"Ever since I can remember, I have seen colors in connection with people. I do not remember a time when the human beings I encountered did not register on my retina with blues and greens and reds gently pouring from their heads and shoulders. It was a long time before I realized that other people did not see these colors; it was a long time before I heard the word 'aura,' and learned to apply it to this phenomenon which to me was commonplace. I do not ever think of people except in connection with their auras; I see them change in my friends and loved ones as time goes by—sickness, dejection, love, fulfillment—these are all reflected in the aura, and for me the aura is the weathervane of the soul. It shows which way the winds of destiny are blowing."

Once Cayce realized that this phenomenon was unusual, but in no way peculiar to him, he began comparing his own impressions with those of other people. He found them surprisingly in accord. "We only differ with regard to the colors which are in our own auras," he said. "This is curious, for it shows how universal are nature's laws. We know that opposites attract and likes repel. Well, I have a lot of blue in my aura and my interpretation of this color does not always jibe with that of a person whose aura does not contain it and who therefore interprets it objectively. One lady I know has a great deal of green in her aura, and she is inclined to dislike green in the aura of others, and place a disagreeable interpretation on it, whereas it is the color of healing and a fine one to have."

Cayce was able to see personal characteristics of perfect strangers reflected in their auras. But he found it best, in terms of being helpful, to know the individual. "Then I can tell him when I see the twinkling lights of success and achievement, or warn him when melancholy or illness threaten. Of course I do not do this professionally. I would not think of such a thing. But I believe it is an ability which all people will someday possess, and therefore I want to do what I can to get folks used to the idea of auras, so they will think in terms of them, so they will begin to attempt to see auras themselves.

"Where do the colors come from, and what makes them shift and change? Well, color seems to be a characteristic of the vibration of matter, and our souls seem to reflect it in this three-dimensional world through atomic patterns. We are patterns, and we project colors, which are there for those who can see them."

Cayce had been asked, during the course of a reading ten years earlier, to give the nature and source of an individual's aura.

"Auras are twofold," the reading said. "That which indicates the physical emanations, and that which indicates the spiritual development. These, when they are kept more in accord with the experience of individuals, make for greater unification of purpose and ideal.

"The aura, then, is the emanation that arises from the very vibratory influences of an individual, mentally and spiritually—especially from the spiritual forces."

Even earlier, the sleeping Cayce had described the aura as "not a cause, but a result—the result of a condition existing within the entity. By 'entity' we mean not just the physical being or body, but the whole being, including the mental and spiritual being."

Elaborating on this, he had said, "As we react to various conditions, we emanate or send out certain vibrations. . . . We ourselves throw off energy, since we are constantly building and have built within ourselves. Our reactions are radiations which form themselves into color. That which we as individuals radiate, or throw off as energy, is the aura."

Over the years, Cayce worked out a kind of color chart to explain the meanings of colors as seen in a person's aura. These are based on his own experience with reading the auras of those around him, comparing what he saw with what other people who shared this particular talent saw, and noting the relationship between colors seen in a person's aura and events and conditions in this person's life that seemed to match the aura patterns.

As an example, he told of a man he'd known from boyhood who had always worn blue. "Frequently," Cayce said, "I have seen him with a blue shirt, blue tie, and even blue socks. One day he went into a store to buy some ties. He was surprised to find that he had selected several which were maroon in color. He was even more surprised when as time went on, he began to choose shirts with garnet stripes and ties and pocket handkerchief sets in various shades of scarlet. This went on for several years, during which time he became more nervous and more tired. He was working too hard and eventually he had a nervous breakdown.

"During this time the red had grown in prominence in his aura. Now gray, the color of illness, began to creep into the red, but as he recovered, the gray disappeared and then the blue began to eat up the red. Eventually all the red was consumed and he was well. Nor did he ever afterward wear anything red, scarlet, or maroon." Apparently, then, a person reacts to his own aura by the choice of his clothing colors, even if he is not aware that he *has* an aura!

Cayce felt this was not at all uncommon. "The majority of people do see auras, I believe, but do not realize it. I believe anyone can figure out what another person's aura is in a general way, if he will take note of the colors which a person habitually uses in the matter of clothing and decoration. How many times have you said of a woman, 'Why does she wear that color? It does not suit her at all.' How many times have you said, 'How beautiful she looks in that dress. The color is just right for her. She was made to wear it.' In both cases you have been reading an aura. The first woman was wearing a color which clashed with her aura. The second woman was wearing a color which harmonized with her aura. All of you know what colors are helpful to your friends, and bring out the best in them. They are the colors that beat with the same vibrations as the aura, and thus strengthen and heighten it. By watching closely you can even discover changes in your friends as they are reflected in a shift in the color predominating in their wardrobe."

Here, in an abbreviated version, is the color chart developed by Edgar Cayce.

Red

Red indicates force, vigor and energy. Its interpretation depends upon the shade and, as with all colors, upon the relationship of other colors. Dark red indicates high temper, and it is a symbol of nervous turmoil. A person with dark red in his aura may not be weak outwardly, but he is suffering in some way, and it is reflected in his nervous system. Such a person is apt to be domineering and quick to act. If the shade of red is light it indicates a nervous, impulsive, very active person, one who is probably self-centered. Scarlet indicates an overdose of ego. Pink, or coral, is the color of immaturity. It is seen usually in young people, and if it shows up in the aura of one who is grown it indicates delayed adolescence, a childish concern with self. In all cases of red there is a tendency to nervous troubles, and such people ought to take time to be quiet and to get outside themselves.

Orange

Orange is the color of the sun. It is vital, and a good color generally, indicating thoughtfulness and consideration of others. Again, however, it is a matter of shade. Golden orange is vital and indicates self-control, whereas brownish orange shows a lack of ambition and a don't-care attitude. Such people may be repressed, but usually they are just lazy.

Yellow

Golden yellow indicates health and well-being. Such people take good care of themselves, don't worry, and learn easily. Good mentality is natural to them. They are happy, friendly, and helpful. If the yellow is ruddy, they are timid. If they are redheads they are apt to have an inferiority complex. They are thus apt often to be indecisive and weak in will, inclined to let others lead them.

Green

Pure emerald green, particularly if it has a dash of blue, is the color of healing. It is helpful, strong, friendly. It is the color of doctors and nurses, who invariably have a lot of it in their auras. However, it is seldom a dominating color, usually being overshadowed by one of its neighbors. As it tends toward blue it is more helpful and trustworthy. As it tends toward yellow it is weakened. A lemony green, with a lot of yellow, is deceitful. As a rule the deep, healing green is seen in small amounts, but it is good to have a little of it in your aura.

Blue

Blue has always been the color of the spirit, the symbol of contemplation, prayer, and heaven. Almost any kind of blue is good, but the deeper shades are the best. Pale blue indicates little depth, but a struggle toward maturity. The person may not be talented, but he tries. He will have many heartaches and many headaches, but he will keep going in the right direction. The middle blue, or aqua, belongs to a person who will work harder and get more done than the fellow with light blue, though there may be little difference between them in talent. Those with the deep blue have found their work and are immersed in it. They are apt to be moody and are almost always unusual persons, but they have a mission and they steadfastly go about fulfilling it. They are spiritual-minded for the most part, and their life is usually dedicated to an unselfish cause, such as science, art, or social service.

Indigo and Violet

Indigo and violet indicate seekers of all types, people who are searching for a cause or a religious experience. As these people get settled in their careers and in their beliefs, however, these colors usually settle back into deep blue. It seems that once the purpose is set in the right direction, blue is a natural emanation of the soul. Those who have purple are inclined to be overbearing, for here there is an infiltration of pink.

White

The perfect color, of course, is white, and this is what we are all striving for. If our souls were in perfect balance then all our color vibrations would blend and we would

72

have an aura of pure white. Christ had this aura, and it is shown in many paintings of Him, particularly those which depict Him after the resurrection.

*   *   *

These are handy guidelines for those of us who now see, or hope to see, colors in connection with people we know. As one who has always experienced this phenomenon, I can assure you that it is most helpful to be able to detect, in a loved one, the warning signs of impending illness (always gray), or that flash of red that says, "Tread softly; this person is upset about something!"

As might be expected from one so psychically talented as Cayce, however, his view of an aura was a great deal more complex. He was able to study the aura in terms of the position of the colors contained in it, their intensity, and how they were distributed. As Cayce saw it, "The aura emanates from the whole body, but usually it is most heavy and most easily seen around the shoulders and head, probably because of the many glandular and nervous centers located in those parts of the body."

He saw the aura in specific shapes. "In children, for instance, it is possible to tell whether a great deal of training by example will be needed, or whether precept will do as well. If the child is reasonable and will accept instruction on this basis, the aura will be like a rolling crown. If example is needed, the aura will be a more definite figure, with sharp points and a variety of colors. If the child intends to be a law unto himself, the aura will be like a rolling chain, lower than the position of a crown, going about the shoulders as well as the head."

Cayce went on to say that several times he had seen little hooks of light dotted through a person's aura. "In each case, the man had a job as overseer of large groups of other men, a director and a leader."

To Edgar Cayce, the perception of color and light around each person he met was a natural phenomenon—so natural, in fact, that the absence of an aura meant one thing: imminent death. But to most of us, such perception is not natural at all, although Cayce felt it could be developed. "You can become color-conscious," he said, "and you can learn to read auras from people's clothes and the colors you see predominant in their surroundings.

"It can be a fascinating game, noticing how any person with vitality and vigor will have a little splash of red in a costume, in a room, or in a garden; noticing how persons who are quiet, dependable, sure of themselves, and spiritual, never are seen without deep blues—it is almost as if they turn things blue by being near them. Notice how bright and sunny people, who like to laugh and play, and who are never tired or down-hearted, will wear golden yellow and seem to color things yellow, like a buttercup held under the chin.

"Colors reflect the soul and the spirit, the mind and the body, but remember they indicate lack of perfection, incompleteness. If we were all we should be, pure white would emanate from us. Strive toward that, and when you see it in others, follow it as if it were a star. It is. But we who must take solace from smaller things can draw comfort from blue, get strength from red and be happy in the laughter and sunshine of golden yellow."

CHAPTER EIGHT

PSYCHIC DEVELOPMENT IN OTHERS

Who among us, at one time or another, has not wished for the power to see into tomorrow? Who among us, at one time or another, has not wished for the power to understand what lies beyond that mysterious condition we call death? Who among us, at one time or another, has not wished for the power to know, as clearly as if spoken aloud, the thoughts and desires of another person? And, through knowing, to be able to *will* the thoughts and desires of another to conform to our own?

Who among us has not, at one time or another, experienced what seemed to be a genuine manifestation of ESP? A dream that later comes true; a statement by one person "heard" by another person moments before it is spoken; a positive kind of feeling that something is going to happen, that does happen, just the way we knew it would—all these things, and many more, convince us of the reality of ESP and psychic phenomena.

Now, suddenly, it seems that everyone is talking about ESP, and haunted houses, and the significance of dreams. A scientist writes an article for a national magazine concerning his discovery that plants can be affected by the emotions of human beings, and appears on the Johnny Carson television show to explain this, and demonstrates the elaborate equipment by which he learned this to be so—and wonder of wonders, this man is not laughed off the stage! A famous clergyman and an equally famous psychic medium appear in a nationally televised seance in which contact may have been made with the clergyman's dead son—and if the results of the seance are not fully understood or accepted by all, at least they are accorded respectful attention.

Suddenly, everyone wants to know more about this kind of thing. Maybe, just maybe, there is something in it after all!

Certainly there is no longer a lack of printed information about the subject. Hundreds of books and articles are being published every year, including the book you now hold in your hands, in which people tell about their own psychic experiences or those of others. Many of these books go further: they tell the reader how to develop psychic ability in himself.

We who have long studied psychic phenomena are gratified that at last we can talk openly about our subject without too much fear of ridicule. We welcome careful and thoughtful experimentation in the field. At the same time, we are somewhat alarmed by some of the advice being given on the subject of developing psychic ability. People are being taught the principles of automatic writing, of self-hypnosis, and more; indeed, many well-meaning individuals are *urging* them to learn these things. But we wonder if such matters are not being grabbed up a little too enthusiastically for the good of some of the people involved.

Perhaps we should pause, then, and consider what the Cayce readings—and Cayce consciously—had to say on some aspects of psychic phenomena.

Clairvoyance and Telepathy

Funk & Wagnalls Standard Dictionary defines telepathy as "the supposed communication of one mind with another at a distance by other than normal sensory means; thought-transference."

Edgar Cayce, in one reading, stated, "Be sure of this fact; be assured of this: thought-transference occurs when both bodies, or entities, are in the subconscious condition—whether for a moment or whether for ages. For time in spiritual forces is not as it is in material forces."

Funk & Wagnalls Standard Dictionary defines clairvoyance as "the ability to see things not visible to the normal human eye; second sight . . ."

Edgar Cayce, in one reading, stated, "*Every* entity has clairvoyant, mystic, psychic powers." This theory was advanced in many Cayce readings.

At another time he said, "In the study of phenomena of this nature there should be, first, the analysis as to purpose. . . . What is the source of the information . . . that goes beyond . . . ordinary . . . guessing? What is the basis of telepathic or clairvoyant communication? What are these in their elemental activity?

"To be sure, this experience is [in] a portion of the mind; but mind, as we have given, is both material and spiritual . . .

"It is not, then, to be a calling upon, a depending upon, a seeking for, that which is without, outside of self; but rather the attuning of self to the divine within, which is a universal, or the universal, consciousness . . .

"As to making practical application—it is what you do with the abilities that are developed by this attunement in coordinating, cooperating one with another in such experiment. For the universal consciousness is constructive, not destructive in any manner, but ever constructive in its activity with the elements that make up an entity's experience in the physical consciousness . . .

"The more each is impelled by that which is intuitive, or the relying upon the soul force within, the greater, the farther, the deeper, the broader, the more constructive may be the result.

"More and more, then, turn to those experiments that are not only helpful but that give hope to others, that make for the activity of the fruits of the Spirit.

"Wait on the Lord; not making for a show, an activity of any kind that would be for self-glorification, self-exaltation, but rather that which is helpful, hopeful for others."

Edgar Cayce discussed this in a public address on February 15, 1931. In part, this is what he had to say:

"Mind reading, or mental telepathy, does exist; we know that. We experience it ourselves every day. Many of us have had the experience of thinking about someone—and that person calls us on the phone. Again, we may have been speaking about certain people, and they walk in the door.

"This kind of thing happened to me just a few days ago. We were discussing a subject. As far as I knew, there was no reason on earth for the person involved to come to my home; but as we were speaking of him and his abilities, it happened that he appeared right then.

"What caused this? Was it chance—just an everyday occurrence? Or was it that the thought-vibrations between our minds and his mind brought about the conversation?

"My experiences have taught me that practically every phase of [psychic] phenomena may be explained by activities of the subconscious mind." [Author's italics.]

Cayce then related an experiment in mental telepathy which he had carried out some years before, while he was still working as a photographer. He told his assistant, a young woman who had discussed various phases of psychic phenomena with him on many occasions, that he could will a person to come to him. She thought this would be impossible, and said so. Cayce then challenged her to name two people she felt could not be influenced in this way.

"You couldn't get my brother to come up here," she said. "And I know you couldn't get Mr. B to come here, either, because he dislikes you."

"I told her," Cayce related, "that before twelve o'clock the next day her brother not only would come up to the studio, but he would ask me to do something for him. And the day after that, before two o'clock, Mr. B would come, too."

At about ten o'clock the next morning, Cayce entered the studio and sat quietly thinking about his assistant's brother. "I felt sure he would come," he said. "I did wonder, though, if I hadn't overstepped myself in saying he was going to ask me to do something for him, because his sister had told me he didn't have any patience with the work I did."

After thirty minutes of meditation, Cayce looked out the window and saw the boy passing by on the street below. "He stood there a few seconds, looking up the steps—then walked away. In a few minutes, he turned in again and came up the steps to the second floor."

The sister looked around and said, "What are you doing here?"

The boy sat on the edge of the table, turning his hat around in his hands. Then he blurted out, "Well, I hardly know—but I had some trouble last night at the shop, and you've been talking so much about Mr. Cayce, I just wondered if he couldn't help me out."

The next day, Cayce repeated the experiment with Mr. B as the target of his thoughts. He sat quietly for about half an hour and then left, telling his assistant that he preferred not to be in when Mr. B arrived, ". . . because he dislikes me so much."

Afterwards, the young woman reported that at twelve-thirty, Mr. B had indeed come into the studio. She had asked him if there was anything she could do for him.

"No," he snapped. "I don't know what I'm doing here. I just came up!" Looking puzzled, he turned and marched out.

Cayce then told his audience that he had never repeated the experiment, and never would. "Now, to my way of thinking these are examples of mental telepathy, or mind reading—but they show a forcing of yourself upon some-one else. That's dangerous business! It pertains to the black arts; it's one of those things none of us has a right to do unless we are very sure of what we're doing, and of our motives. Sometimes it might be used well, perhaps at times to control our children in that way. Yet even then it might be dangerous, for, as our information says, anyone who would force another to submit to his will is a tyrant! Even God does not force His will upon us. Either we make our will one with His, or we are opposed to Him. Each person has an individual choice.

"Then what part may mental telepathy play in our lives—that is the big question. For anything good can also be dangerous. I could mention nothing good but what it also has its misapplication, its misuse. How, then, may we use mind reading or mental telepathy constructively?

"The best rule I can give is this: don't ask another person to do something you wouldn't do yourself. The Master never asked such a thing; and let us never ask it."

Once, in giving a reading, Cayce addressed himself to whether or not the combined thought power of many individuals could change the course of physical events. He stated, "We find that when the thought of many individuals is directed to one focusing point, the condition becomes accentuated by force of thought manifested . . .

"As thoughts are directed, the transmission of thought waves gradually becomes the reality—just as light and heat waves in the material world are now used by man. Just so in the spiritual planes the elements of thought transmission, or transference, may become real."

Automatic Writing

The practice of automatic writing has long been of interest to students of psychic phenomena. Often Cayce was asked, during the course of the reading, to advise on this subject.

Once he was asked if it is possible to communicate with entities in the spirit plane by means of automatic writing. He replied, "Yes. By practice. Sit alone with pencil and paper and let that guide that may be sought, or may come in, direct. It will come. Anyone may do this—*but is it the better way?* It may oft be questioned."

Cayce always cautioned against possible dangers to the individual when engaging in automatic writing. In a reading given in 1938 he said, "We would not, from here, counsel *anyone* to be guided by influences from without. For the Kingdom is from within! If these come as (automatic) inspirational writings from within, and not as guidance from others—that is different."

In 1936 he urged another, "As has been indicated, rather than automatic writing or a medium, turn to the voice within! If this then finds expression in that which may be given to self in hand—by writing—it is well. But not that the hand be guided by an influence outside of self. For the Universe—God—is within. Thou art His. Thy communion with the cosmic forces of nature, thy communion with thy Creator, is thy birthright! Be satisfied with nothing less than walking with Him."

Hypnosis

Hypnosis, in the hands of a responsible therapist, can be one of medicine's greatest allies. In spite of all the stage demonstrations, and attendant hilarity, it continues to be studied seriously as a safe and efficient means of relieving both physical and emotional pain.

It should be pointed out, here, that *all* hypnosis is, in effect, self-hypnosis. No one can control the subconscious mind of another. What happens is that a receptive subject will accept the suggestion of a skilled therapist and hypnotize himself. At no time is the subject "taken over" by the therapist.

I once witnessed a dreadful demonstration of unthinking hypnosis that illustrates how dangerous it can be under the wrong conditions. The hypnotist, an amateur who had nevertheless worked many times with the subject of this experiment, was showing the process to a number of us following a dinner party. We were sitting around the living room in a friend's house in Mount Clemens, Michigan. The hypnotist put his subject "under," and gave her the suggestion that she was in a room in a Swiss chalet. If she would go to the window, he said, she would see the skiers getting ready for their day on the slopes. He described the scene outside the window, as well as within the room; his subject indicated that she saw everything he described. She seemed to be having a thoroughly enjoyable time; looking through the window at Michigan's September-red hills, she exclaimed over the beauty of the snow.

The hypnotist said, "If you'd like to join them, go get your skis from the bedroom."

His subject turned immediately, and with some excitement started for the door to the hall. Just as she stepped across the threshold, she sank to the floor and began crying hysterically.

It took us some time to figure out what had happened. But the answer was simple. The hypnotist, you'll recall, had said, "You are in a *room* in a Swiss chalet." The moment she stepped through the door she was back in the house in Mount Clemens, and her disappointment was crushing. It was several days before she completely recovered from the experience.

Hypnosis is discussed in a great many Cayce readings. Cayce's first concern, in prescribing it, was the person who would be administering it. Most often it was not a professional hypnotist, but a member of the patient's own family who was to give the suggestion.

Once he was asked, in connection with a 13-year-old boy who was a deaf-mute afflicted with epilepsy, "Could hypnotism be used in this case?" He answered, "It might be used, but be mindful of who would use same!" He advised that autosuggestion would best be given by the boy's mother.

He was asked, then, to give the form of suggestion to be used. He replied, "That as is desired to be awakened. Work with one applying the manipulative (osteopathy) forces in this, but appeal always to the inner being—that being awakened in this formative period of the development of the body, mentally and physically. This may be as a form, but should be put in the words of the individual making such suggestions. [Say,] as the body sinks into slumber, 'May the self, the ego, awaken to its possibilities, its responsibilities, that, as I speak to you, in the normal waking state you will respond in that same loving, careful manner that is given to you.' See?"

In a reading for a young woman suffering from insanity, Cayce indicated that the suggestion should be given by "one of the people that have a clean mind themselves. The body is good to look at and it would not be well to put under the influence of one with ulterior motives or desires." [Note the clairvoyance indicated by the expression "good to look at." Cayce had never, consciously, seen this patient.]

For a man who had been suffering from constant hiccoughs for six days, Cayce prescribed hypnosis. "Let this be done by suggestion, through such as Kahn."

And finally, this general statement on hypnosis. "Many an individual, many a personage has given his all for the demonstrating of a truth.

"As it has been indicated from the first—through this channel, there should ever be that ideal, 'What does such information which may come through such a channel produce in the experience of individuals? Does such make them better parents, better children, better husbands, better wives, better neighbors, better friends, better citizens?' And if and when it does not, *leave it alone!*"

Possession

We have discussed several areas in which people are experimenting with what we might term "do-it-yourself psychic development," and we have given you a general summary of Cayce's advice concerning them. Hugh Lynn Cayce, in his book *Venture Inward*, has told of his personal observations of people who got themselves into trouble as a result of injudicious experimentation along these lines.

We now come to the most startling concept of all: the possibility that there can be such a thing as possession.

Does this idea—yes, in the old-fashioned sense of the

word, meaning that a human being has been "taken over" by the spirit of some discarnate entity—bring a smile to your lips? It may well do so. After all, a lot of gripping suspense stories have been built around this subject. It is such a far-out idea, with such exciting ramifications, that it makes good fiction. Therefore, it is difficult to consider it seriously.

The sleeping Cayce, however, did consider it seriously. We have no way of knowing whether or not he was correct in his statements about it, but the subject came up in many readings. Bearing in mind the high rate of accuracy of his physical readings—which will be discussed a little later in this book—we can only offer you the following examples and invite you to make of them what you will.

Once, reading for a 72-year-old woman, Cayce said, "Yes, we have the body here." He paused for a long moment, and then said in an undertone, "We have possession here."

Reading for a woman who had questions for Cayce regarding the problems of her alcoholic husband, he was asked, "What causes my husband to lose control of himself?"

Cayce answered immediately, "Possession!"

"What is meant by possession?"

"Means POSSESSION!"

To the next question, "Is he crazy or mentally deranged?" he replied, "If possession isn't crazy, what is it?"

"Does possession mean by other entities, while under the influence of liquor?"

"By other entities while under the influence of liquor," replied the sleeping man. "For this body, the husband, if there could be a sufficient period of refraining from the use of alcoholic stimulants, and the diathermy electrical treatments used, such treatments would drive these entities out! But do not use electrical treatments with the effects of alcohol in the system; it would be detrimental."

We have given these examples to show that, to Cayce, possession was something that might happen to anyone. For those experimenting with such activities as automatic writing and self-hypnosis, however, the need for special caution was indicated throughout the Cayce readings.

Here are three cases dealing with the consequences of careless experimentation with certain Yoga techniques. [This does not, by the way, include Yoga exercises used to improve physical health; Cayce often recommended these in his readings.]

In a reading for a 50-year-old woman, Cayce said, "While those activities that have been taken by the body produce some conditions that are beneficial . . . they have caused and do assist in producing the exciting of the glandular forces in their activity, as related to the genital system. This, combined with pressures upon the nerve system, [causes] distorted and disturbing conditions for this body."

"What causes the burning sensation which comes over me, as if someone has [put] the power on me?" he was asked.

"This is the incoordination between the cerebrospinal and the sympathetic nervous systems. And as the glandular system is affected—as related to the genitive system, and epecially affecting directly the center above the puba—there is produced (with the toxic forces in the system) this burning, and the *effect of possession!*"

"Should anything be taken for the glands?"

"As has been indicated, there has already been too much taken!"

In a reading for a woman of 53, Cayce said, "The body is a supersensitive individual who has allowed itself—through study—through opening the gland centers of the body, to become possessed with activities outside of itself . . ."

"How did I happen to pick this up?"

"The body—in its study—opened the gland centers, and allowed self to become sensitive to outside influences."

"What is it exactly that assails me?"

"Outside influences. Discarnate entities."

And finally, for a 39-year-old woman, Cayce said, "There has been the opening of the lyden gland, so that the kundaline forces move along the spine to the various centers that open—with the activities of the mental and spiritual forces of the body. The psychological reaction is much like that which may be illustrated in one gaining much knowledge, without making practical application of it. . . . Now combine these two and we have that indicated here as a possession of the body—a gnawing, as it were, on all of the seven centers of the body, causing the inability to rest or even [engage in] a concerted activity, unless the body finds itself needed for someone else. Then the body finds, as this occurs, the disturbance is retarded or fades, as the body exercises itself in giving help to others."

We know this sounds fantastic. But we do not apologize for offering it here. After all, who's to say Cayce *didn't* know what he was talking about?

We should take a moment to explain some of the terminology used in the above readings, or connected with it in some way, for it may be completely unfamiliar to you.

Kundalini is a Sanskrit word for an activity connected with Yoga. By concentrating on nerve centers, and through exercise and breathing, kundalini, a fundamental power of electrical force, may be awakened in the body. Unless done under expert supervision, it is considered a dangerous practice. Probably some of the people mentioned in the above readings had been experimenting with this activity without utilizing proper controls.

Kundalini is believed to lie at the base of the spine, coiled like a serpent, until deliberately raised up through the various chakras in order to radiate from the top of the head.

Chakras (another Sanskrit word) are seven vortices of psychic energy. They are said to be situated along the spine and in the head, and are considered, in Yoga, to serve as points of reception for "pranic forces" (vital energies) which rouse the individual to action. They are psychic in nature, not physical. Beginning at the base of the spine and working up to the head, their corresponding glands—which *are* physical, of course—are the adrenals, the sex glands, the pancreas, the thymus, the thyroid, the pituitary and the pineal glands.

In the last-mentioned reading above, for the 39-year-old woman, Cayce mentioned that there had been "the opening of the lyden gland, so that the kundaline forces move along the spine to the various centers that open . . . ." *Lyden gland* was a term used often by Edgar Cayce in his readings, to designate the source of Leydig cells. These are interstitial cells which secrete the androgens or male hormones.

In a reading given in September, 1928, Cayce stated, "The basis or seat of the soul is in the lyden (Leydig) gland."

This is a confusing statement. "Lyden gland" does not appear in any dictionary or in any of the endocrine charts I consulted, and I examined many of them. Leydig cells *are* recognized, of course—and accepted scientific knowledge seems to agree with what Edgar Cayce had to say on the subject. Did Edgar Cayce suffer a slip of the tongue *on the great many occasions* when he mentioned the lyden gland, or did he have access to some very special information—information just waiting to be discovered, or rediscovered?

In one reading, Cayce stated, "Lyden, meaning sealed, is that gland from which gestation takes place when a body is created . . . located in and above the genital glands." Here, too, he said, "The base or seat of the soul is in the lyden (cells of Leydig)."

So the readings indicate that the soul enters the body through the cells of Leydig, or the lyden gland. They also suggest that the soul continues to function through a network connecting gland tissue in various portions of the body. As one reading explained this, "The spiritual contact is through the glandular forces of creative energies; not encased only within the lyden gland of reproduction, for this is ever—so long as life exists—in contact with the brain cells through which there is the constant reaction through the pineal."

In the early 17th Century, the French mathematician and philosopher, Rene Descartes, identified the pineal gland as "the seat of the soul." He based this theory on the belief that the pineal was found only in humans. When it was discovered to exist among other vertebrates —sometimes proportionately larger than in humans —Descartes' theory was pretty much laid to rest. However, many Cayce readings refer to the pineal gland in just these words; and in one reading it was referred to as "a channel through which psychic or spiritual forces may manifest."

If there has ever been an orphan among glands, it is

certainly the pineal. A tiny organ attached, like the pituitary, to the base of the brain, it lost its status as a "gland" when—after intense research failed to locate a pineal hormone—scientists began to refer to it as the "pineal body." Indeed, the pineal seemed of no value at all to the human body.

Then in 1958, a hormone, melatonin, was isolated from the pineal. Scientists connected with this advance were quoted as saying, "It is possible that the pineal gland has a function not yet discovered." With the discovery of melatonin, the word "gland" was restored to the pineal.

Somewhat later, experiments were conducted at Harvard Medical School with a protein-free extract from the pineal glands of beef cattle. Administered by injection to a group of fifty-five chronic schizophrenics, there was improvement in each case—and results in some cases were said to be "spectacular."

In a reading given in 1932, replying to a question concerning the source of his information, Edgar Cayce said, "There must be, in the physical or material world, a channel through which psychic or spiritual forces may manifest. . . . In this particular body [Edgar Cayce] through which this at present is emanating, the gland known as the pineal gland, with its thread, is the channel along which same operates. With the subjugation of the consciousness—physical consciousness—there arises, as it were, a cell from the creative forces with the body to the entrance of the conscious mind, or brain, operating along, or traveling along, that of the thread or cord [called by Cayce, at times, the silver cord] as, when severed, separates the physical, the soul, or the spiritual body."

In another reading he said, "Pituitary forces become manifest in intuition.

"In the body we find that which connects the pineal, the pituitary, the lyden, may be truly called the silver cord . . . which is the Creative Essence in physical, mental and spiritual life; for the destruction wholly of either will make for the disintegration of the soul from its house of clay."

And, at another time, "It [the pituitary] is the door . . . through which physically all of the reflex actions [penetrate] through the various forces of the nerve system. It is that to and through which the mental activities come that produce the influences in the imaginative system as well as the racial predominating influences—or the blood force itself.

"In the spiritual it is that in the adult which brings the awakening to its capabilities, its possibilities, its ultimate hope and desire.

"In the mental it is that which gives judgment and understanding, tolerance and relationships to the determining factors . . ."

"Why Do They Doubt?"

In a general reading, given for the purpose of getting information about psychic phenomena, Edgar Cayce was asked the question that has plagued all who seriously study the subject, "Why do so many people ridicule the idea that useful information can be obtained through this source of psychic data?"

He replied, "Lack of understanding of the law governing so-called psychic powers; lack of consciousness being brought to the individual of the potential powers which are manifested in and through the psychic or occult forces.

"Much of this misunderstanding is caused by the lack of proper use of the knowledge obtained through such sources. For the incorrect use of such knowledge may, and would, bring destructive elements . . .

"The only real life is that which, in the material or physical plane, is called psychic. . . . Those who ridicule such forces are to be pitied rather than condemned, for they must eventually reach that condition (adversity, frustrations, etc.) wherein the soul awakens to the elements necessary for the developing.

"For without the psychic force in the world, the physical would be in that condition of 'hit or miss,' or as a ship without a rudder or pilot. For that element which is the guiding force in each and every condition is the spirit or soul of that condition—which is the psychic or occult force."

CHAPTER NINE

TELEPATHY AND/OR CLAIRVOYANCE AS SHOWN IN THE PHYSICAL READINGS

The sleeping Cayce "practiced" a strange kind of medicine, in that it recognized no boundaries. If osteopathy was indicated as being best for the particular body, and for the particular ailment, then an osteopath—often specified by name in the reading—was recommended. If surgery seemed the only solution, then surgery it was—and again, the M.D. to perform the operation might be named. Odd medicaments were often recommended; so odd, in fact, that many times they had to be specially compounded of ingredients named in the reading. Occasionally the dose seemed poisonous in nature or in proportion. Then the druggist filling the "prescription" might quietly substitute another ingredient for the one called for in the reading. (In such cases, the next reading would confirm what had happened, as an explanation for the patient's not having improved or become completely well.) Often, in the case of a psychosomatic disorder, Cayce offered a special prescription for cure: that of getting the mental and emotional house in order.

The Cayce physical readings, in short, form a curious amalgamation of naturopathy-osteopathy-surgery-drugs-psychology-diet therapy. The only limits, it seems, were dictated by the needs of the patient. Since Cayce, in trance, was constrained by the dictates of no particular order or school of medicine, he was free to suggest whatever each patient required to get well.

However, before others—and Cayce himself—could become convinced that what he was doing in his readings was not only harmless, but actually beneficial, they were used almost exclusively on people closest to Cayce, and then only as a last resort. Indeed, an examination of the family history almost makes it appear that desperate situations were thrust on Cayce as a means of forcing him to use his psychic ability. Each time he tried to turn his back on the power that had been given him, he was impelled by circumstances to return to it once again.

One of many such instances was the case of his wife, Gertrude, who contracted tuberculosis soon after the birth, and death, of their second son. The physicians attending her gave her up to die, just as her brother had died from the same disease.

Cayce, still trying to make a career as a photographer, and still questioning the value and safety of the information that was coming to him when he went into the unconscious state, gave a reading for her. The diagnosis, according to the physicians, was excellent. So was the general statement of her condition. However, they said, the suggested treatment was truly ridiculous. They admitted that the diet matched the one customarily used for TB patients. But she was to take drugs—including heroin, mixed to make a liquid and administered in capsule form—which were normally used to make up prescriptions; never should they be taken in the form Cayce had specified in the reading. Hardest of all to take seriously, though, was the recommendation that Gertrude inhale the fumes of apple brandy contained in a charred oak keg!

So the doctors refused to have anything to do with it. The local druggist risked jail by making up the compounds called for in the reading without benefit of a doctor's prescription. The apple brandy keg was procured, and treatment was begun in August, 1910. By January, Gertrude was well on her way to complete recovery.

Edgar Cayce "Cures" Edgar Cayce

Probably it was the strain of this period in their lives that resulted in a reading given on December 1, 1910, for Edgar Cayce himself. It dealt with the vocal paralysis which afflicted him periodically throughout his adult life. Whenever emotional or physical strain proved to be too much for his body to tolerate, Cayce would become unable to speak above a whisper.

The reading was conducted by Al C. Layne, the Hopkinsville, Kentucky, amateur hypnotist (and correspondence school osteopathy student) who had discovered, in 1900, that although Cayce would not respond to the posthypnotic suggestions of others, he was capable of following his own when in a self-induced trance. (It was Layne, too, who had discovered that Cayce could also prescribe treatment for the ills of others. Layne gave the name "readings" to this activity of Cayce's unconscious mind.)

In the reading, Cayce was asked to examine the throat of the body, Edgar Cayce, and ". . . tell what is the matter with it, if anything."

Cayce replied, "The muscles of the vocal cords here, you see, produce a partial paralysis to the vocal cord, especially to the left side of the vocal box. You see, the cords are taut from the box or sound here, as the air is expelled from the lungs . . . We have a nervous effect of the nerves and muscles all over the whole body; we have a tightening or a sensation in the nerve force to contract it and of the muscles of the vocal cord or box here.

"All along in the front part of the body along the larynx to the vocal cord, to the right end here in front, this muscle is taut; then the voice sounds as if it is loose here, or not contracted by the nerve forces and muscles. Together, this leaves one side that does not sound and produces a whispering sound. This comes from the same trouble we have had before from the pelvis."

"What will we do to remove that now?" asked Layne.

"Just circulation here will remove it; that is the only thing that will do it. Suggestion to the body forces the circulation through it here, and as the circulation passes along it takes that away—puts new life to it—makes the supply to the nerve force go, you see."

Layne gave the suggestion, as he had done in the past: "Increase the circulation and watch that and see the condition removed; that congested condition. Increase the circulation. Is that removing now?"

"Circulation is beginning to increase," said Cayce. [It should be noted that while this was going on, his voice was normal. Without the procedure being followed in the reading, however, it would have reverted to a mere whisper upon awakening.]

Layne continued the suggestion. "Watch it increase, now. Watch that remove. All that congested condition will be removed away by the circulation. Passing off now, is it not?"

"Passing off now," said Cayce.

"Watch it move clear on; it will become normal. Will be in its normal condition. Watch it now and when that becomes perfectly normal, tell me."

Cayce replied, "Have to remove the trouble first."

"What is the trouble now? You see the trouble is away. Now the trouble is gone. Now the vocal cords are perfectly normal, are they not?"

"They are perfectly normal now."

"That is all right now," said Layne. "They will continue to work perfectly. Now at times in the past, he [Edgar Cayce] has suffered with severe headaches. What causes the headache?"

"In the pelvis."

"How will we remove that?"

"To operate on it."

"In what way?"

"Here, from the side here."

"Cannot it be done by manipulation?"

"Cannot absorb it. It has hardened at times past, you see; it is hard. See here the testicle comes—here at the upper end of the pelvis—comes in contact with a lesion at the second lumbar, and there you see it forms a lesion. Now between this lesion and into the pelvic region here—right opposite to the left side and about two inches from the pelvis bone—has formed a clot or a knot at the time of cold or extreme excitement or anything [that affects] the nervous organism of the system. It produces then the pains that revert to the head, at the top, in the center. Produce cold all along the spine and heat on top of the head. When we reverse this it settles in the organs; that is, in the weakest point in the system. These come together again from these troubles in sympathy with the sympathetic system here at the stomach. We have at times, at the same time, a filling up of gases in the stomach; pains in the lower part, in the intestinal tract. We have a reverse and produces the condition in the intestinal tract itself. That is the aftereffects and not the cause of the trouble. The trouble is from the clot that formed here from this accident we have had here in the testicle.

"It will have to be here. Roll the intestines to the side; we have here at the lower part a clot formed and when that is cut loose it makes a reaction to the nerve supply and makes it rebuild instead of forming this clot on the nerve force here."

Layne gave the final suggestion before the one to wake Cayce. "Your circulation is going to continue perfect."

Now, what do we find in this reading? Many things.

First, there is the information that Cayce's vocal paralysis was principally of psychological origin. He described the condition, and requested that Layne make the suggestion that the circulation increase to the affected portion. Cayce, amenable to such a suggestion, then proceeded to do so!

Gladys Davis (Turner), Cayce's secretary for many years, witnessed this phenomenon many times. Upon being given the suggestion, she has reported, Cayce's face and throat would change in color from normal to deep pink, as the circulation was increased. After the skin color had returned to normal, Cayce would announce, "The condition is removed." When he came out of the trance, his voice would be perfectly normal again.

There is also, in this reading, information concerning Cayce's headaches and intestinal pain. It was stated that the pain resulted from an accident involving a testicle, which had caused a clot to form in the intestinal tract—causing, in turn, an obstruction which must be removed by surgery.

Cayce, when this reading was completed, reported that he *had* suffered such an accident; in childhood, he had fallen on a stick which had gone completely through the testicle. It was a serious injury and healing was painfully slow.

The condition was completely verified a few years later, when Cayce was operated on for appendicitis. The surgeon reported that he had never seen a worse case. Cayce's intestines were terribly twisted and obstructed, just as the reading had indicated.

The Aime Dietrich Case

As we have mentioned, the first readings, with a few exceptions, were given for members of the Cayce family.

One of these exceptions concerned Aime Dietrich, and it occurred in August, 1902. Edgar Cayce, who was then working in a bookstore in Bowling Green, Kentucky, was summoned to his home town of Hopkinsville one Sunday to deal with the seemingly incurable case of a little five-year-old girl.

According to her father, the child had been perfectly normal up until the age of two, when, following an attack of influenza, her mind had simply stopped developing. A great many specialists had been consulted, but none had been able to provide the answer or even stop the convulsions which were coming in increasing numbers— sometimes as many as twenty a day. Her father had heard of Cayce through Al Layne, and was now turning to him as a last resort.

Cayce found, when he entered the Dietrich nursery, a beautiful child with an absolutely blank mind. A nurse stood by, watching Aime's every move. Edgar Cayce wondered if he had a right to tamper with this child's life by asking for information from a source he couldn't begin to understand. It was not an easy decision. However, he reasoned, what *other* chance did she have?

So he gave the reading. It indicated that, a few days prior to coming down with influenza, Aime had suffered a fall which had injured her spine. (Her mother later confirmed this. Aime had slipped when getting out of the family carriage and fallen to the street. But she had jumped right up, seemingly unhurt, so her mother had thought no more of the accident.) The flu germs had settled at the site of the injury, said the reading. It was this, and this alone, that had caused the trouble. Instructions were given for some osteopathic adjustments, which Layne would administer.

For Layne, a "mail order" osteopath without benefit of diploma, some additional readings were needed to be sure that he was giving the proper adjustments. He did make some mistakes, and the readings were careful to point these out and suggest correct procedures.

Within a matter of weeks the child's mind had begun to pick up where it had left off three years before. Within three months she had managed to make up for most of the time lost to illness and had caught up with children of her own age. She recovered completely, and developed just as normally as if nothing serious had ever touched her life.

The case of Aime Dietrich has been reported by many of Cayce's biographers, and is therefore well known. So we have not disguised her name or any of the circumstances. However, in discussing other cases in this book, fictitious names will be used to protect the identities of the people for whom readings were given. This is in accordance with A.R.E. policies; although the files are open to the public, they have been carefully coded for this purpose.

The Strange Pregnancies of Wilma Franklin

Some warnings concerning possible future trouble were given in a reading for Wilma Franklin on September 3, 1937. She was twenty-six years old, and had been married just under a year. Her doctor had assured her that she was not pregnant, and she had taken some pills to bring on her overdue menstrual period.

Severe abdominal pains, fever and hemorrhage followed. Her mother-in-law, utilizing an old family remedy of some kind, applied a large quantity of iodine to Wilma's abdomen in the belief that it would relieve the pain. Wilma's husband called Edgar Cayce's office, several hundred miles away, and requested an emergency reading.

Cayce began it with one of his frequent demonstrations of clairvoyance. "We find the odor of iodine about the body."

He then proceeded to outline the case in full, explaining, ". . . as we find, conditions that disturb in the present are acute, arising from the organs of the pelvis, or more specific the sac, there being produced or caused spasm in same—by the active principles of orris and ergot—and an expulsion of the activities of the system from normalcy." In other words, it was the pills that had caused the trouble—and Cayce had named a couple of ingredients. Unfortunately, we are unable to attest to the accuracy of this.

"For it is as serious as an abortion would be," he continued. "Unless there are great precautions taken in the activities of the body, it will be very hard for the body to have the period of gestation without a great deal of trou-

ble, and the inability to carry through the full periods."
(From the events that later occurred, as we shall see, it
seems that Wilma may well have been pregnant, after all,
and that the drug had caused an unwanted abortion.)

Wilma was told, in the reading, to keep off her feet for
at least ten days, to keep her hands out of cold water (a
frequent and somewhat mystifying Cayce warning in
such cases), to have some osteopathic manipulations "to
correct adjustments in pressures from the lumbar, sacral
and coccyx area," and to watch her diet and eliminations.
Cayce cautioned that the uterus had "dropped down" and
must be allowed to return to its proper position, principally through sufficient rest and reclining, in order that
future pregnancies might come to term.

Two check readings were given during the next several
days. On September 7, Cayce urged Wilma to remain off
her feet. On September 14, he stated that improvements
were being made and that Wilma might begin to be a little
more active, "but not too strenuous for the next several
days."

On September 19, a reading stated, "Conditions are not
so well as we last had same. Too much activity has caused
a bruising through the pelvic area and thus brought on the
flow again." Cayce suggested that curettage might be required, and upon a request to do so, named the doctor to
perform it. It was done the next day by the physician
named in the reading.

On September 27, Cayce began another check reading
with a psychic weather report, "It is raining there!" [Wil-
ma later confirmed this.]

The reading indicated that "conditions are progressing, in the main, very satisfactorily." Again he suggested
more attention to proper eliminations, the use of a
specifically named tonic, and "two or three more
osteopathic adjustments . . . not so much now for the pelvic organs as for the head and neck and the drainings from
same to the alimentary canal." [Wilma was also having
trouble with her ears at this time, although Cayce's office
had not been told of this.]

On April 5, 1938, a Cayce reading for Wilma Franklin
indicated that she was pregnant. However, said the reading, "Conditions are not yet wholly normal. Then, there

96

will be the necessity of being very careful during this period; keeping off the feet most of the time, hands out of water to any great extent, keeping the feet very warm—and most of the time when resting, the lower limbs should be a little bit elevated, see?"

Menstrual periods had continued in spite of the pregnancy, and the reading indicated that, should this continue after the third period, hospitalization would be required. Also, said the reading, the womb had dropped —a serious complication. Osteopathic adjustments were recommended, and were outlined specifically.

In a reading on April 20, Cayce said, "Conditions as respecting the attempt to save the body-developments are rather serious. . . . The organs of the pelvis are out of position and in such a state of strain that the fetus forces are causing a drainage that produces irritations, as well as a great deal of pain. It is, of course, close to the third month, as indicated. Hence it becomes the more serious for all conditions."

Wilma was advised to contact Dr. G, a surgeon, and be hospitalized immediately. This was done.

On May 7, Wilma's husband wrote to Edgar Cayce. "Wilma has been getting along fine since Dr. G fixed her up. I was pretty much worried about her for a while. Thanks a million times for the readings."

On May 24, Wilma wrote to Cayce, expressing her own gratitude. She added, "Needless to say, I'm so excited about this coming event of ours that I can hardly realize that it is actually true. I think I'm about straightened out now. . . ."

On June 6, another reading was given. It stated, "While there are disturbing conditions at times, especially at the periods, gestation is being carried on in near to a normal way and manner. . . ." Caution was ordered; Wilma was to walk a great deal, but avoid any strenuous activity. A specific cod liver oil and iron tonic was recommended. In the reading, upon request, Cayce supplied the name of the physician to see Wilma through her confinement, Dr. H.

A letter dated July 21 from Wilma to her mother, who lived in another state, indicated that some rather peculiar things were going on. In the first place, although according to the Cayce readings Wilma was now in her sixth month of pregnancy, no one—including any of the doctors—was convinced she was really pregnant. She continued to have her menstrual periods on schedule, didn't "look pregnant at all," and felt fine, she said.

"Even Dr. H isn't positive," she went on. "He is very interested in the information from 'that fellow Cayce,' as he calls him. He practically asked me to get another reading to 'see what he'll have to say about it. He's done some wonderful things; maybe he can throw some light upon this case.' The quotations are his. He's funny—terribly interested in the readings but doesn't want to appear too much so. He was completely flabbergasted when I told him that I had come to him through advice from a reading from Mr. Cayce. I didn't say anything about my reading the first time I went to him, since I didn't know his ideas on the subject. But during the second visit, while he was trying to make me understand, in a very diplomatic manner, that I was more than likely mistaken about being pregnant and was giving me that pregnancy test to top off his opinion, the conversation gradually came around to the point where I could introduce the subject.

"He remembered Dr. M [a doctor who had worked closely with Cayce in the past] and in that way, finally, I got to the point I wanted. I let him do the talking and he was going strong. He said, 'You know that fellow has really got something; I don't know what, but something.' Said he met him only once, years ago, and knew of several things about him. Says he has been interested for a long time in such subjects and liked to talk about them, but that you just couldn't talk about such things, 'because people will think you're nutty.' He expressed it just that way and it just seemed so odd to hear Dr. H talk like that. He doesn't strike you as a person interested in psychic matters. Anyway, he's interested in my next reading. . . ."

In a letter to Edgar Cayce a few days later, Wilma told of her experiences with Dr. H and his attitude toward the readings. "It was while we were waiting for the results from a pregnancy test (an injection in my arm) that I told him I'd had a reading and that it said I was pregnant. He was very much interested and waited enthusiastically for the results of the test. The test *agreed* with what the reading said and he pulled on his nose several times real hard and said, 'Well, it looks like the ole boy is right.' That was the second visit to him. I've been several times since, and he still isn't convinced in his own mind about it. He said, 'Well, if Cayce says you are pregnant, I suppose you are. But you couldn't prove it by me!"

On July 29, another reading was given for Wilma, in which some questions she had included in her letter to Edgar Cayce were asked. The reading indicated that Wilma's condition seemed good "in many directions. However, if there is the continued strain produced upon the system, as well as upon the fetus—through the drainages from the system through the [menstrual] periods, there will not be allowed normal or nominal developments. . . ." X-rays were suggested, with extreme care to protect the fetus, in order to determine the safety of allowing the pregnancy to continue. "The conditions and the tests, from the very natures that have existed, would show that there are not normal conditions, not a normal pregnancy."

In answer to the question concerning how far advanced Wilma's pregnancy was at this time, Cayce said, "The condition is advanced as has been indicated [about six months] but the development of same—as to the proportions and all—is less than a month in size or form, or not more than two months." Rather alarming news for Wilma in *that* reading, we'd say!

Her letter to Edgar Cayce, on August 8, informed him that she had taken the reading to Dr. H. "It was the first one he'd ever seen, and the expression on his face as he read it was an experience! He has felt all along that I'm not pregnant—but allowed for the possibility that he might be wrong. He read it over and over and said finally, 'I just don't know what to make of it. It sounds logical, but I can't understand why I can't locate this evidence if it's there."

X-rays, according to Wilma, had been made; they showed nothing. "He gave me a thorough examination, too, and he couldn't find any symptoms of pregnancy. He said, though, that there was only one thing to do and that was to wait and see what developments took place. . . . Dr. H gave me the enclosed questions to ask in my next reading. He admits the possibility of the fetus removing itself in a natural manner if it is not to develop normally. He said that he believes that is what will happen if I really am pregnant, if it hasn't happened already.

"This is the strangest sort of experience. We never dream such things can happen to *us*. And I feel so good physically. Naturally I'm worried, and I tire much more quickly than usual—but aside from that I still feel grand."

The next reading took place on August 11, 1938. It began, "Now, as we find, conditions have not changed since that as last we had here. Under the existing conditions, we find that the interpretation should be rather first by those handling the condition [Wilma's doctors]. For to interpret and then not be assured by their own indications or findings will only make for confusions.

"Conditions are much as has been indicated, as we find. There has been inception, not once but more than once —as has been and is indicated by the blood test, as well as the character and the profusion of activity of the glandular system.

"That there have continued to be first conception, then abortion, then conception and then abortion, has made for the abnormal developments.

"But the construction and the developments must be followed by those handling same [the doctors].

"Ready for questions."

The conductor asked the questions, speaking for Wilma. "Am I still pregnant at this time?"

"At this time still pregnant—about six to ten weeks; and this added to others makes for this shadow that is indicated."

"What is the cause of continual menstruation?"

"Continual abortion!"

"Will the fetus develop in the normal manner?"

"Not until some changes have been made—and there is a retaining and a normal development of the flows of the system for nominal or normal developments."

"How shall we interpret the X-ray picture which we have made?"

"Use the common sense!" Cayce paused for a moment, and then ended the reading with the usual phrase, "We are through."

Wilma wrote to Cayce on August 14: "Thank you

100

again. It is very upsetting, all this, in view of the fact that the doctors think I'm not pregnant. Nothing else showed up in the X-ray. The two shadows I asked him about when I first saw them were, he says, a little gas in the intestines! It shows a shadow about the size of a silver dollar, and a much smaller one a little distance from the larger one. 'Gas in the intestines' it *is*, as far as they're concerned. They think I've tried to *think* myself into a state of pregnancy! Can you imagine?

"I haven't had a chance to show this latest reading to Dr. H. I hope to see him today. It may make a difference in his opinion . . .

"The abortions the reading described were the two very unusual [menstrual] periods which I've experienced, evidently. Dr. H didn't think it important. But I've been in bed each time never less than a week; sometimes ten days to two weeks. That was taking place and I didn't know it!"

Wilma Franklin was indeed pregnant, in spite of what her doctors had to say about it. She miscarried a few weeks later, and there was no question that it was a true miscarriage.

After all her trouble, we are happy to report that, in a letter to Edgar Cayce dated April 3, 1939, Wilma stated, "I have beautiful news. We're expecting a baby in early fall, and are so happy about it. I'm getting on fine and feel grand and am sure there won't be any trouble. However, I'd like to be positive about it and will sincerely appreciate it if you will [give me] a check reading when you can arrange it.

"I haven't been to a doctor yet. I can't help feeling hesitant about them after my experience last summer. I just don't feel very confident about any of them and am sincerely in a quandary as to whether or not to go back to Dr. H. I'd like to ask that in the check reading."

The reading, given on May 9, stated, "As we find, conditions are developing normally.

"There should not be any hindrance towards full, normal development, if there is plenty of exercise taken . . ."

A few osteopathic manipulations were recommended, "not for corrections, other than assisting the body in correcting its new positions—but for relaxing of the system, for the bodily forces to adjust themselves to the develop-

101

ment of those conditions with the body." A special cod liver oil and iron supplement was recommended, as well as a calcium preparation.

Concerning Wilma's reluctance to consult the doctor who had attended her before, Cayce said, "The physician we would continue; Dr. H should care for same. While this in some respects offers—mentally—some disturbing conditions, we find that as to abilities, other than Dr. T—there's not a better one in this vicinity; and one that may be relied upon, if all conditions are thoroughly understood."

In answer to specific questions, Cayce replied that the baby was developing normally, and that a maternity supporter should be worn "when the time comes. Fitted by the [osteopath] would be advisable." As to a question about exercise, "Do as has been indicated. Do not over-do, but keep plenty of exercise. Don't try to jump or dance or the like, nor kick up the heels, but plenty of walking, plenty of keeping in the open. . . ."

In a letter dated May 21, Wilma thanked Cayce for the reading. "I'm so grateful to know that I'm getting on so well. Of course I knew, as far as it's possible to know, that everything was progressing normally, but the readings 'see' things that the rest of us can't know. . . .

"That's funny, the reading sending me back to Dr. H. He'll like that. He was very pleased at being recommended last summer. I'll explain to him, too, what [the reading] meant by 'disturbing conditions' regarding him. I *do* have confidence in him; I was just peeved at his attitude!"

A check reading was given on August 26. Conditions, said Cayce, were quite normal. "There should be the expectancy, as we find, between the first and the eighteenth of September."

Cayce then gave a weather forecast! "Owing to circumstances as will arise, not of the physical but of natural forces—the weather—it would be better if the body would be in the hospital rather than at home. . . ."

Actually, he missed the date of delivery by some two weeks. The baby, a girl, was born on September 29 with no complications. The weather forecast, however, was completely accurate. The sudden cold snap that occurred while Wilma was in the hospital proved too much for her home heating system, and it broke down!

Wilma's second child, a boy, was also a "Cayce" baby. The reading, given on November 30, 1942, indicated that delivery could be expected on July 10 or 11. Cayce's batting average improved with this one; the baby was born on July 16!

It is interesting to note that Wilma had suffered a miscarriage only a month before conceiving this child, who was born eight and a half months after the reading was given. So perhaps Cayce's earlier readings, indicating that Wilma's miscarriages were followed almost immediately by other conceptions—a highly unusual situation—were not nearly so farfetched as they might have seemed at the time.

The Case of the Missing Light Ray

Alice Marshall was suffering from a severe mastoid infection. A reading was given on April 21, 1928, which supplied the diagnosis and recommended treatments. Three days later, a check reading was given.

Cayce began, "Yes, we have the body here. This we have had before. Now we find in many ways the body shows improvement from that we have had before; yet there is the indication of reinfection, especially in the area about the soft tissue in the inner ear, and that in the portion just back of ear. Would there have been applied the light ray—that affects the nerve and blood—we would have found a different condition, as we see it."

A letter from the person attending the patient carried the confession that the light ray had indeed been omitted from the treatment because of fear that it would burn the skin. Following the second reading, the light ray was applied. The patient's recovery was swift and complete!

A Case of Poisoning

Janet Baylor, at 8:20 in the morning of January 21, 1940, was extremely sick.

It had begun at about 8:30 the night before, with all the signs of acute indigestion or food poisoning. The first attack of pain and diarrhea had resulted in fainting. About ten o'clock the family physician had been called; he had administered a hypodermic injection which had relieved Janet for a few hours. The second attack had then come,

103

worse than the first, and the doctor had returned to give her a second injection. At that time he had advised immediate surgery for what he felt was locked bowels. A third attack, he said, might well prove fatal.

Janet had refused surgery—at least for the time being. But since six o'clock that morning she had been vomiting about every twenty minutes. Her father went to the Cayce home to sit in on the emergency reading, which was given at 8:20 A.M.

Mrs. Cayce, conducting the reading, said, "You will give the physical condition of this body at the present time; giving the cause of existing conditions, also suggestions for help and relief of this body, answering questions that may be asked."

"Yes," said Cayce. "We have the body. This we have had before.

"As we find, the acute conditions arise from the effects of a poison—Pyrene.

"From this activity the acute indigestion as produced through the alimentary canal has caused an expansion of, and a blocking in, the colon areas.

"As we find in the present, we would apply hot castor oil packs continuously for two and a half to three hours.

"Then have an enema, gently given. It would be well that some oil be in the first enema; that is, the oil alone given first, see? Olive oil would be better for this; about half a pint; so that there may be the relaxing.

"And then give the enema with body temperature water, using a heaping teaspoonful of salt and a level teaspoonful of baking soda to the quart and a half of water. Give this gently at first, but eventually—that is, after the period when there has been the ability for a movement—use the colon tube.

"Then we would take internally—after the oil packs and the enema—a tablespoonful of olive oil.

"This, as we find, should relieve the tensions and relax the body sufficiently to remove the disturbing conditions . . . ."

At the end of Cayce's instructions, he was asked to supply the source of the poison. "Pyrene," he said. "Pyrene—on the beans!"

This was later explained by Janet. She had been visiting

104

her mother the day before the reading, a few hours before the illness struck. In late afternoon she had fixed herself a raw vegetable cocktail, using her mother's new juicer, and one of the ingredients was a handful of "some beautiful green string beans."

There were no laboratory tests to confirm that Pyrene had been the cause. And it is not clear how Pyrene—trade name for a carbon tetrachloride preparation used in fire extinguishers—might have found its way to the green beans consumed by Janet Baylor. Possibly it was through some industrial accident, or an accident during shipping of the vegetables.

At any rate, if Cayce was correct in his reading, it had been enough of a dose to make Janet a very sick girl. From her symptoms, there was little doubt that it was a true poison, and the lengthy recuperative period indicates that it was a serious one. But she did avoid surgery, and she did get well.

"Treat the Cause, Not the Effect"

The case of Mary Lewis is one of the most extraordinary, and one of the best-documented, to be found in the Cayce files.

To fully appreciate the value of Cayce's clairvoyance in this instance, it is necessary to know a little of Mary's case history.

A schoolteacher in New York City, Mary had gone to Florida in the fall of 1935, at the age of thirty-two. In March, 1936, she was discovered to be suffering from advanced tuberculosis. She spent the next three months in a Miami hospital, during which time pneumothorax surgery (artificial collapse of the lung by the injection of air into the pleural cavity) was performed on each lung. In June, 1936, she returned to New York and entered Bellevue Hospital. Pneumothorax treatments were continued. Sputum tests indicated the tuberculosis was still active. An X-ray report in July indicated, according to the attending physician, "about twenty-five percent collapse of upper lobe of right lung. Adhesions at the apex. The cavity below clavical not collapsed. The uncollapsed portion of the lung shows nodular infiltration, fibrosis and coalescence of the lesions, most marked in the middle third of the lung. Similar changes in lower half of the left lung."

In September, Mary was transferred to Sea View Hospital in Long Island. Pneumothorax continued; surgery was considered by several of the specialists attending the case. An X-ray report on September 2 indicated, "Bilateral pneumothorax present. There is a nominal amount of fluid in the right base and extensive collapse of the lung, the apex of which is still suspended from the upper chest by numerous band adhesions. There is a large cavity in upper lobe, immediately beneath site of adhesions. There is a peripheral collapse of left lung which shows no definite excavated lesion, but there does appear to be an acinous nodose seeding throughout the lower two-thirds."

At the end of September, Mary entered Manhattan General Hospital in New York City, where surgery, intrapleural pneumolysis on the right lung, was performed. She remained there, confined to bed, for six weeks. Pneumothorax treatments were discontinued in the left lung but continued in the right. X-rays following surgery indicated that the cavity, due to pressure, was closed to some extent. Adhesions and extreme pressure on the right lung had pushed the sternum and heart toward the left side of Mary's body, crowding the left lung. Breathing was extremely difficult, and any movement of the body was nearly impossible.

By November, Mary's finances were exhausted, and her emotional state was poor. She returned to her parents' home in Virginia. Placed immediately in a tuberculosis sanitarium nearby, she remained there until a few days before the Cayce reading was given on March 12, 1938. At the time of her release from the sanitarium she was told that her tuberculosis had been arrested, but that she would have to continue pneumothorax in the right lung indefinitely. She was to spend nearly all her time in bed; and the doctor attending her warned her parents that Mary would most likely be bedridden for the rest of her life. He expected to have her back in the sanitarium soon —possibly to stay for good.

Her parents had heard of Edgar Cayce, and arranged for a reading. Mary was allowed to attend the session; but she asked specifically that Cayce not be told anything about her case before the reading.

He began the reading by getting immediately to the point. "Now, as we find, the conditions and the causes of same are rather specific. The *effects* of the disturbances have been the more often called the *causes,* rather than that which is producing same.

"These are affectations to the pulmonary circulation and the associations of the activities of the disturbances there upon the rest of the system.

"However, as we find, the causes arise from pressures which exist in the cerebrospinal system; and—through the deflected nerve portions of the system—have thickened tissue, producing pressure upon the capsule of the lung.

"Thus we find the disturbance and inflammation caused, rather than infectious forces arising *only* through being predisposed to disturbance through the pressures . . . ."

Cayce then proceeded to give a complete rundown of Mary's condition, including information about the blood, the nerve system and, finally, clinical details concerning the state of her throat, bronchi, larynx and lungs.

One of the most important statements in the reading, however, was, "This was caused first by the inhalation of foreign substance, dust and the like. Then with the pressure produced by an injury in the area indicated, there was caused—or begun—the disturbance there."

Detailed instructions were given regarding diet, exercise, osteopathic manipulations and rest. In addition, Mary was to use the apple brandy keg so often specified in Cayce readings for TB.

"First, have prepared a cask or keg—gallon or gallon and a half, oak, charred inside. If it is a gallon keg, put in same half a gallon of apple brandy. Not apple jack but *pure apple brandy.* Keep this tightly corked but close to where it will produce evaporation. Prepare so that the gases may be inhaled; not the brandy but the gas *from* the brandy; inhaled through the mouth into the bronchi, larynx and lungs. Do this at least two or three or four times a day."

With faithful attention to all the instructions given in the reading, said Cayce, "We should, within six to eight months, be entirely free of the disturbance for this body."

When the reading was over, Mary talked for a while with Gladys Davis, who had taken stenographic notes of all that had been said by Cayce.

"It's incredible!" she exclaimed. "I haven't thought of it for years, but I know exactly what injury Mr. Cayce was referring to—the one that led to my TB. You see, about fifteen years ago I fell from a tree and hurt my back, up near the shoulders. For over a week I was in such pain that I had to stop teaching. I went to an osteopath and had a couple of treatments. The pain left, and I returned to my job. I was bothered by it for some time afterwards, but after about a year and a half, the trouble seemed to clear up."

She paused, and began to tick off some dates. "Yes. Eleven years after that accident, I was in charge of a settlement house in New York City. I worked outdoors in the recreational field a lot of the time. I was exposed to the dust of the playground, changing weather conditions and poorly ventilated classrooms.

"That's probably when I breathed in the foreign substance, like dust, that Cayce talked about in the reading. I was in that job for two years. Then I went to Florida, where I found out that I had TB."

Finding the apple brandy keg required a month; it is, after all, a rather unique item! However, one was procured, and the treatments began. On June 6, a second reading was given, in which Cayce stated that much improvement in the general condition had been made. He altered his instructions somewhat; due to the excellence of osteopathic manipulations that had been made, he said, these could now be cut down from twice a week to about twice a month.

Following this check reading, no further pneumothorax treatments were ever required for Mary Lewis—after only two months of actual treatment under the Cayce regime!

In August, a third reading cautioned against too much activity; by now, Mary was feeling so well that she actually had to be restrained from overdoing things!

In December, Cayce gave a fourth reading for Mary, in which he said that "conditions are much improved. Much lung tissue has now been renewed, and is working

108

well—even aids [the body] rather than being a detriment to it."

Continuing, he said, "The keg is as life itself. When it is prepared again, rinse it out first, you see, before it is refilled again. Rinse with warm—not hot, but warm —water, so that the accumulations from the distillation or evaporation of the properties are removed, and there is less of that influence or force which arises from the acids that come from such infusions." As always, there was no detail of treatment too unimportant to be fully explained.

The next reading was given on January 4, 1940, less than two years after Mary's first reading. Cayce reported that although "to be sure, the weaknesses and the inclinations as yet exist, as indicated by the tendencies of portions of the right lung to settle . . ." there were no "live tubercular forces through the system, or through the lung area. There are no more adhesions of the pleura."

At this time, Mary reported that she had seen the doctor who had released her from the sanitarium a year and a half earlier, expecting to have her back as a bed patient within a matter of weeks. His reaction to her appearance, she said, was one of amazement. "He asked if I had got religion, since that would be the only explanation he could find for the continued and marked improvement!" X-rays and tests, of course, confirmed the conditions Cayce had described in his reading.

In November, 1941, the final reading was given for Mary Lewis. "The conditions are good," reported Cayce. "While there are still indications of affected areas, there are not indications of the areas being active."

Mrs. Cayce, conducting the reading, said, "Please read the last X-ray, which I hold in my hand."

Cayce unhesitatingly did so. "We find that this indicates there is not active tissue in the area that *has* been the disturbing center; that there is not *any* adherence in any of the wall of the pleura; that there is a good flow of circulation throughout all portions of the lungs themselves save in that one particular area." [Accuracy of Cayce's clairvoyant reading of this X-ray: 100 percent, according to the attending physician.]

Cayce reported that Mary would now be able to return

to work—so long as it did not overtire her body; preferably she should work out-of-doors.

Reports from relatives to A.R.E. tell what has happened to Mary in the years since her readings were given.

In 1952, her mother reported that, during 1942, Mary had used the keg ". . . mostly on those occasions when she had a cold. Her health was pretty good and she was enthusiastic about her progress. At about this time she met Mr. Andrews, and was instrumental in getting a reading for him. As suggested in his reading, he took one or two osteopathic treatments. After that, he discredited the value of both the treatments and their source.

"In 1943 they were married. By that time, my daughter had discontinued all treatments outlined in her readings. I was very much concerned about her, because I had heard that she and her husband drank occasionally. Financial difficulties gradually developed, and by 1945, my daughter had turned to strenuous outdoor work to help with the income. As the strain of their marriage relationship increased, they both resorted more frequently to alcohol. My daughter became very nervous, irritable and neurotic.

"In 1947 she had a cyst removed from her rectum. About two years later, a second operation was performed for the same condition. She became extremely thin and her face looked pale and drawn. Eventually her marriage ended in a separation. And yet, none of these hardships caused TB to return.

"Today, while she is still a neurotic addicted to drink, she has nevertheless good resistance. She has gained weight and looks well. I am indeed grateful that, all things considered, at present she is free from tuberculosis."

Later reports to A.R.E. from Mary's sister indicate that, although other illnesses have been experienced through the years, there has been no recurrence of tuberculosis. In 1967, she said that Mary is quite well. She is no longer bothered by a drinking problem, and her mental attitude is excellent.

A Question Not Asked, But Answered

Kim Albright, just two years old, had been sick for the past week. Her parents wrote to Edgar Cayce, requesting a reading. They volunteered no information concerning her condition, and submitted only two questions: (1) What is causing the digestive disturbances, and (2) How can we protect her from the infantile paralysis epidemic now raging in this area?

Cayce, in his reading, stated, "From outside influences we find that pressures have been caused in the cerebrospinal system; especially in the areas of the second and third dorsal and third cervical, which has caused some deflection to the activity of the stomach, as well as a deflection in the auditory forces—which is indicated in the speaking voice.

"This should be corrected, else we may find—while it may be corrected in a manner by the body's own growth—it would leave weaknesses and tendencies to be met later on, in the digestive system as well as in the abilities of enunciation. . . ."

So Cayce had detected, at a distance of some nine hundred miles, that this child—who had been talking quite well since the age of eighteen months—had suddenly developed a severe case of stuttering!

Cayce was asked, in the reading, "Was this pressure from an injury, or just what?"

He replied, "From the outside, apparently from a wrenching or hitting—or wrenching of the spine. Of course, it was very slight, but it has been sufficient to deflect even the emptying of the duodenum."

This reading was given in September, 1941. Upon seeing it, the child's aunt recalled that in June, while visiting friends in another town, Kim had fallen off a couch, "right on her head. She didn't seem badly hurt, so we didn't pay any particular attention to possible injury. Probably that's what jammed all those vertebrae mentioned in the reading."

Osteopathic treatments were started at once, and the child recovered completely.

Too Long a Wait

Much more than telepathy was at work when Edgar Cayce, at Virginia Beach, gave a reading for Don Collier, a small boy in an Ohio hospital, in October, 1942.

The case had been diagnosed as polio. This seemed the most probable answer to the doctors, who had noted some paralysis on the right side of the boy's body for about a month.

Cayce, however, said, "These are very serious disturbances; a form of strep that, unless this is allayed, will attack the brain or nerve [spinal] cord structure itself."

The child's temperature at the time of the reading, said Cayce, was 103° [This was confirmed later as being exactly right.]

Cayce gave his instructions, which included—of all things—a crushed grape poultice to be applied over the abdomen.

Apparently a good deal of precognition was involved in this reading. In addition to the remark about the strep eventually attacking the brain or nerve cord, Cayce said, "*If* there is improvement, then we may give further instructions on Friday or Saturday." Unfortunately, the child died later that day, too soon for Cayce's "prescriptions" to be tried.

The postmortem disclosed that the case was not polio. It was a form of strep that led to meningitis—in other words, the germ did attack the spinal cord and brain. Perhaps, if the doctors had known what the disease really was, if the reading had just been requested a little sooner
• • • •

A Word for the Skeptics

It is easy to find reasons for the high percentage of "cures" among the Cayce files. Certainly there were some people who were suffering from psychosomatic ailments, or even overactive imaginations, who needed only to believe that Cayce could make them well in order to *become* well. The readings themselves, over and over, indicated the importance of mental attitudes and emotions as they relate to bodily health.

But then you come across correspondence such as this, a report from a woman given to A.R.E. in 1952, referring to her husband's physical reading in July, 1943, and you begin to wonder.

The reading began, "As we find, these conditions have gradually grown to be of a very serious nature. The crystallization of the segments, or the cartilaginous forces

112

in the segments of the spine, have become gradually so taut, from the accumulations because of lack of eliminations from the body, that this stiffness in the lumbar and lower dorsal area is almost static. . . ."

Although the reading was five pages long, no name was given to the ailment. As so often appears in the Cayce readings, it was not names that mattered, but manners of treatment. These Cayce gave in this reading, in complete detail, with some criticism of the way the case had been handled by others.

At any rate, this is how it all came out, in the words of the wife. "The doctors said there was a parathyroid tumor and tuberculosis of the kidneys. Later X-rays revealed that this was not correct. [The doctors] indicated that there was no hope, and that my husband would eventually turn to jelly. There was nothing they could do, they said. They suggested that he take aspirin.

"I knew that the things Mr. Cayce gave would work, but my husband did not. I literally overrode his objections in carrying out the treatments.

"My husband was not at all keen on the treatments, but I continued to give them to him just as outlined, for I was sure they would work.

"He continued to improve, although after 1945 he only kept up the treatments occasionally and paid attention to the general diet that had been outlined for him in the readings.

"When the doctors would meet him on the street, later, they would turn white with the shock of realizing that he had not died. They asked him to come in so they could check him and see what the changes were. He did not want to do this, and I did not encourage him to do so, because there were so many unpleasant memories connected with his previous illness.

"He is now enjoying the best of health—boating, swimming, dancing and carrying on his business."

At the time of this report, this man—who didn't really believe the Cayce readings could do much for him—was sixty-four years old and still going strong, nine years after he'd been given up for nearly dead.

This brings up a thought-provoking question. If he had

no faith in Cayce's work, and followed the readings only because his wife insisted on it—then what, pray tell, made him well?

It's the Attitude . . .

Leona Masters, after reading Tom Sugrue's biography of Edgar Cayce, *There Is A Rver,* in June, 1944, wrote to Cayce for help. "I have been in three hospitals and treated by many doctors, but only one doctor has made a suggestion as to what he thinks it may be. He said that my symptoms came nearer to indicating disseminated lupus erythematosus than anything else, and that if such is the case, the only thing that medical science can propose is rest, and keep out of the sun. I've been resting and keeping out of the sun ever since I went to the hospital in November, but the disease is still with me. At the last hospital the doctor said that I did not have that disease, but they didn't have any idea what disease I *did* have.

"The illness began in October, and I was in bed from November to April, and then spent the month of May in bed. I am stronger now and have no fever at present, but the disfiguring eruption is all over my face and neck. . . ."

The letter, of course, was not given to Edgar Cayce prior to his reading. Nevertheless, he gave a complete and accurate description of Leona Masters' affliction, and added much that was not implied by anything stated in her letter.

One statement in particular is worth noting. At the end of the prescribed treatment, he added, "These, as we find, offer the better prospects. It's the attitude the body takes. Don't attempt to shield self from anxieties but know there are truths, there are conditions one must conform to for bettered improvements through the body, as well as the applications to bring better conditions."

Now, why would Edgar Cayce give advice such as this?

A clue to the desperate need for it came with Leona's next letter to him. She sent a detailed description of what she had been through, emotionally, over the past several months. Her husband had been in a prison camp. She had finally been able to get him back home, but he was not normal mentally.

She said, "The worry, the strain, the constant watching

resulted, I am sure, in my becoming ill with what the doctors considered an unknown disease. Can you believe that not one doctor, of all those who have treated me in three hospitals, has ever asked me if I were worried or had any problems? Since I'd covered up in front of my own family for my husband, I couldn't reveal his condition to a doctor, even though I felt that by talking about the conditions I'd give them a clue that would lead to my recovery. Each time I went to the hospital it was after a fresh shock supplied by my husband. Your reading did take into consideration the mental strain that I was living under—although, as I've said, no doctor ever thought of that angle."

The treatments that Cayce recommended, and the release this woman gained in having someone, somewhere, understand her problems led to a complete cure.

Always the Attitude . . .

Leona Masters was grateful to Edgar Cayce, and profited by his spiritual as well as his physical advice. In contrast we offer the case of Alma Long.

Alma also was troubled by a skin condition. She lived near the Cayce offices, and thus was able to sit in the reading room and listen to what Cayce had to say.

Cayce's secretary reported, "The girl made her appointment for the reading by phone and only appeared at the A.R.E. office a few minutes before the appointed time, talked to me a few moments concerning questions and was ushered into the 'reading room.' It was the first and only time Edgar Cayce saw her. Of course, as usual, he made no conscious 'examination' of the patient."

The problem was clearly outlined in the reading. "There has been a subluxation produced in the eighth and ninth dorsal center, by a strain or a wrench or a hurt. This has caused poor circulation through the areas of the pelvis and from the activities there infectious forces have arisen. These have produced in the lymph circulation a nerve tension and then the body-mind has indicated an unfavorable reaction here. These have brought about nerve tensions which produce, on various portions of the body, a rash, which causes great irritation to the body . . ."

After a full description of treatments to be followed, he added, "Keep as constructive as possible. Don't ever condemn self; don't condemn others! Forgive as you would be forgiven. Keep sweet!"

The readings for Leona Masters and for Alma Long were both given during the month of July, 1944. Both women had come to him as a result of reading *There Is A River*. Their attitudes, however, were quite dissimilar.

There is evidence, in the note from the osteopath who treated Alma, that not much attention was paid to Cayce's spiritual advice. Said the doctor, "My provisional diagnosis was cystitis, pyelitis, dermatitis. I gave her six treatments and had poor cooperation. I am unable to contact her for results. . . . The subluxations were found in the eighth and ninth dorsal." (This, you will recall, is exactly as Cayce had described the situation.)

Precognition—Or What?

In January, 1925, the Cayces were living in Dayton, Ohio. However, on January 16 they were visiting friends in New York City. Around midnight, Cayce was giving a series of readings before a group of people who had assembled to watch him work.

At 12:15 A.M., which would make it early morning of January 17, he finished the readings, and was being given the suggestion to awaken. Instead, he began to speak with unusual urgency.

"Lorraine Whittier. Chicago, Illinois. Now, in this condition that has arisen in the body from the disarrangement in the pelvic organs, especially those in the false pelvis, we find these need attention at once, through that condition as given, for the operation on the body, else there will be in nineteen days the setting up of an infection that will bring destructive forces to the whole system. The alleviation of the pressure has been effective to the body, but this attempt to lift that heavier than the body should have attempted, under the existing conditions, has brought about this condition, or falling more of the organs in the pelvis, and the rupture of the left Fallopian tube, and these conditions should be attended to at once.

"We are through for the present."

This was not the first reading he had given for Lorraine Whittier. However, this was the first one he had given for her *without a specific request*!

116

The Cayces did not return to Dayton for several days. When they arrived there, they found a letter from Lorraine Whittier containing specific questions she wanted answered via a reading.

Her letter was dated January 18, 1925—the day *after* Cayce had given the reading! And yet the reading had answered every question asked in the letter.

Reading From Physical Surroundings

The fact that Edgar Cayce, in trance, could attune his unconscious mind with that of another, and with such exceptional results, is remarkable enough. But consider this: on a number of occasions, when the subject of his reading was away from the location specified in the reading suggestion, Cayce went right ahead and gave his reading anyway—based on impressions from the physical surroundings normally associated with the person!

Such a case is that of Helen Barbour, who was dying of breast and lung cancer. Her friend, Frances Marks, after obtaining permission from Helen's sister to do so, requested a Cayce reading for her. She gave no information about Helen except her home address and the fact that Helen did not know the serious nature of her illness—which, of course, she did not name. When told that the reading would take place at 3:45 P.M. on February 8, 1934, Frances informed the Cayce office that at that time Helen would be away from her apartment, and gave them the two possible locations at which she might then be found.

Accordingly, when the reading suggestion was given to Edgar Cayce, it included Helen's home address, and indicated that at present she would be found either at Radio City or the Medical Center in New York City.

Cayce began speaking. "Yes, we have rather the impressions from the home surroundings, as we have transient conditions as respecting the locating of the body-individual." [Frances Marks explained, afterwards, that Helen had indeed been in transit at that moment.]

The reading proved accurate in every detail, beginning with the first statement. "There are those conditions existent wherein there is tissue in lung, in breast, involved; from conditions where they in their very activity are *creative* from that they produce in the system, or are of the malignant nature—thus not only sapping the life force but filling the blood supply through the character of the condition or the nature of the bacilli so involved throughout the system."

Included in this reading were many provable statements of fact. At times, Helen suffered excruciating pain. Only hypnotics or narcotics were being administered (which, said Cayce, "is to gradually allow the body to lose its resistance or ability for resuscitation"). Also, Cayce indicated, the treatments he outlined in such complete detail "could, and should, be applied by the nurse in charge." Helen was under twenty-four-hour nursing care, and Cayce seemed to know this.

We wish we could report that Cayce's treatments were followed, and that Helen got well, or at least was spared some needless suffering before her death. Unfortunately, such was not the case. As so often happened, her physician refused to cooperate in any way, and continued to give her the only thing medical science had to offer in 1934 for a person with terminal cancer: pain-relieving drugs.

A similar type of reading—that is, one given from the physical surroundings, rather than the body—had taken place a few months before.

It was for a man who told Cayce's office that at the time of the reading, between three and four o'clock in the afternoon of December 5, 1933, he would be on board a dredge in a shipyard in Jacksonville, Florida. If not in the shipyard, he'd be somewhere on the St. John's River near Jacksonville.

As it happened, the man forgot about his appointment, and at the time of the reading was busy in a conference some twenty miles away.

This didn't seem to disturb the reading. Cayce began it by saying, "We have the body associations with the dredge, but we don't find them together." He then proceeded to diagnose the man's back trouble. "The segments in the eighth, ninth and tenth dorsals show a tendency for settling close together, as do the activities of the muscles and the tendons about the sacral and coccyx region.

"These subluxations are not as lesions, as yet, but are rather of the nature that produces, through these areas at times, a dull aching across the hips, through the right side, low down in the caecum area. At other times a heaviness and pain through the upper portion of the body, under the shoulder blades, and a tendency for the mental body to be easily aggravated—or nothing fits just exactly right —making for a lesion in the hypogastric and pneumogastric area, or third and fourth cervicals.

"What areas, then, need adjustment? In the eighth, ninth and tenth dorsals. Relaxations in the lumbar or sacral and coccyx areas."

This man, of course, had not told Cayce anything concerning his condition prior to the reading. He was amazed by the accuracy with which Cayce had described his symptoms.

He took the reading to an osteopath in Jacksonville. As he reported the experience later, "I went right down to her office and said, 'I'd like you to give me an examination. But before you do, I have a letter here I'd like you to read. I want you to read this with an open mind, no prejudice— just pick it up and read it. Don't allow yourself to be influenced by what you read. Then check my body and see how close this comes to what you find according to your science of osteopathy.'

"So she read it and said, 'Well, I've never seen anything like this before.' I then lay on the table and she went down my spine and checked each vertebra. Finally she said, 'It is one hundred percent correct. I find his description is exactly the condition existent.'

"In other words, she found the tautness particularly in the eighth, ninth, and tenth dorsals; it was very pronounced, so that there was no guesswork. Dr. W was astounded when she realized that Edgar Cayce had given that diagnosis from Virginia Beach with me in Jacksonville—and twenty miles away from where I was supposed to be keeping the appointment for him to examine my body. She was actually knocked out; she'd never heard of anything like that."

Osteopathic treatments completely cleared up the trouble.

The man stated, "From that experience I am convinced that we do leave a part of ourselves in places we occupy, say over a period of months, or days.

"There was nothing in that room outwardly indicative of me. My clothes were in a steel locker on the side. There was nothing of me there except the bed I slept on, and, as a matter of fact, the bed had been changed that day. Yet the subconscious picked it up and could tell where the trouble was in the body that occupied that room, even though I had been gone from it since six o'clock that morning. Edgar Cayce gave the reading at three-thirty in the afternoon."

A third case which comes to mind is one that occurred in September, 1929. A woman in New York City had requested a reading, and the time had been set for it.

The readings were delayed that day, however, and by the time Cayce got to it the woman had left her home. He gave it anyway, beginning with, "Now, we do not find the body—but those impressions and *surroundings* of same we find here. . . ."

There is nothing in the reading to indicate that it was not as accurate as it would have been if the woman had been in her home. However, her physical problems were attributed to nervousness and mental attitudes rather than to any organic disturbance.

Perhaps the woman was insulted by this, or somewhat disappointed by the diagnosis. At any rate, she wrote to Cayce in protest. "I fail to see where you could give a reading of my 'surroundings' and expect me to follow suggestions. Therefore, I think I am entitled to another reading . . ."

That Cayce, in Virginia Beach, could put himself to sleep and read her unconscious mind—that she could accept, just as if everyone could do the same thing every day. That he could diagnose her ailments and suggest treatment for them while in this state—that, also, she could accept. But that he could do all this while she was absent from her usual surroundings? Ridiculous!

Human nature—how very wonderful it is!

How Accurate Were the Physical Readings?

In illustrating the clairvoyance of Edgar Cayce as shown in the physical readings, it may appear that we have chosen only those cases in which there was some degree of success, if not *total* success. This has not been deliberate.

However, we necessarily chose those cases in which there was some later contact with the patient, or with the patient's doctor, for these not only bear out the accuracy of the readings, but also provide the most interesting study. There were many readings given for people who were never heard from again. In such cases, it is impossible to determine the accuracy of the readings concerning diagnosis; and it is equally impossible to determine whether or not the treatments were followed and, if they were, whether or not they were helpful.

Of course there were failures. There were times, as we have indicated earlier, when Cayce would put himself into trance, and receive the suggestion from the conductor of the reading, and then lie mute, unable to furnish any information at all. (In most cases, as we've said, later readings would be obtained.) No doubt there were some occasions on which the information received by Cayce didn't apply to the patient—or at least didn't appear to apply to the patient.

As an example of this latter contingency, we might mention one man who has given a reading which indicated that he showed the beginnings of a disturbing and extremely serious blood disorder.

"Poppycock!" he exclaimed. "I just had a thorough checkup, and there's nothing wrong with my blood." He demanded, and received, return of the small fee he'd paid for the reading.

A couple of years later, in the course of checking accuracy of the readings through follow-up letters to people who had been given them, the Cayce office contacted this man's home by mail.

The reply came from the man's wife. "I must answer your questionnaire for my husband. You see, he died six months ago—of leukemia."

The remarkable accuracy of the Edgar Cayce readings, at least those given in connection with physical problems, was confirmed by a survey conducted some years ago by Sherwood Eddy for use in his book, *You Will Survive After Death.*[1]

Mr. Eddy contacted a number of physicians who had treated patients according to the readings. In experience, they ranged all the way from one who had treated five Cayce patients to one who had handled well over a hundred.

Concerning accuracy of diagnosis, estimates were all between 80 and 100 percent correct. Averaged out, this figure comes to a surprising 91 percent.

Concerning treatment, responses again indicated a range of from 80 to 100 percent showing good results. But nearly every physician reported that, where recommended treatments were followed faithfully, there was improvement in *all* cases, and astounding improvement in some. The only failure, according to one respondent, was in the area of cancer.

Considering the fact that a great many people came to Cayce as a last resort, after orthodox medicine had nothing more to offer them, it is hard to believe that the consensus showed nearly 100 percent improvement, if not complete cure!

And Tomorrow We May Discover . . .

There are indications throughout the physical readings that in many ways Cayce was well ahead of his time.

Certainly in the area of psychosomatic medicine Cayce was a ground-breaker. We couldn't begin to cite the number of cases in which proper mental attitudes were stressed, for they were an integral part of the Cayce philosophy, "Mind is the Builder." To Cayce, emotions and mental distress were as much a part of physical illness as any other factor. Just as poor mental attitudes could cause ill health, positive and healthy attitudes could result in good—or at least better—health.

"For what we think and what we eat—combined together—make what we are, physically and mentally,"

[1] Published 1950 by Holt, Rinehart & Winston

said Cayce in a reading given in 1934.

For an eleven-year-old girl in 1943, he said, "But this treatment should be done systematically, expectantly, not doubting! For what ye ask in His name, believing, and thyself living, ye have already."

For a patient suffering from cancer, Cayce once said, "Keep a constructive attitude ever in the prayerful manner." For another cancer patient he said, "The mental attitude has as much to do with the physical reactions as illness in the body."

Anger, said Cayce, "is certainly poison to the system. This should be a warning for every human."

"To be sure," he said in a reading for a young man, "attitudes oft influence the physical conditions of the body. No one can hate his neighbor and not have stomach or liver trouble. No one can be jealous and allow the anger of same and not have upset digestion or heart disorder. Neither of these disorders is present here, and yet those attitudes have much to do with the accumulations which have become gradually . . . tendencies towards neuritic-arthritic reactions. . . ."

We do not mean to imply that Edgar Cayce alone was concerned with the relationship between emotions and physical disorders, or that the concept of psychosomatic illness is new. It is not. But it has been only within the last few decades that medicine has begun to look at the *whole* person, just as Edgar Cayce did in his readings, rather than concern itself merely with one or more malfunctioning organs. This is a great advance, but it also brings a galaxy of complications to the business of determining the cause of any particular disease.

For example: as if the matter of solving the terrible problem of cancer in humans were not difficult enough, there is now evidence that emotions may also play a part in causing it.

This was brought out at a three-day conference sponsored by the New York Academy of Sciences held in New York in May, 1968. One report concerned a study of several hundred cancer patients conducted by a University of Rochester medical team, which strongly suggests that inner feelings of hopelessness and helplessness, caused by the death or separation of a loved one, seem somehow linked to the incidence of cancer.

In addition to this evidence, a New York psychologist conducted in-depth interviews among a group of 500 cancer patients and a group of 500 individuals with no known physical illness. According to this psychologist, the cancer patients' lives were characterized by early loss which brought pain and feelings of desertion, loneliness and even feelings of guilt and self-condemnation.

The conference chairman, Dr. Clauss Bahnson, professor of psychiatry at Jefferson Medical College in Philadelphia, reported that his studies have shown that cancer is most likely to occur in people who are unable to "discharge" their emotions following the loss of a loved one. These unexpressed emotions, said Dr. Bahnson, seem to cause changes in the body's central nervous system which can lower resistance to disease. There was general agreement among many attending the conference that cancer seems to occur most often in those whose immune defenses are down.

Psychosomatic illness, however, was only one area in which the Cayce readings seem extremely advanced for their time.

Polio, now that we have vaccines to prevent it, is on its way out. But during the years the Cayce readings were given, it was a dreaded disease that took a tremendous toll in terms of bodily health, or life itself.

Here, in part, is what Edgar Cayce had to say about polio in a reading given in August, 1936. "From the very nature of the condition, the indications are as a whole that it, the inflammation produced, is of the emunctory and lymph circulation. Hence it is infectious as well as being able to be carried by persons, or it is a carrier disease, also.

"And it arises in the individual from the conditions that exist from what may be termed body infection or bodily-infectious conditions.

"When conditions are at a balance in a body where there is that effluvium thrown off through the circulation and the activity of the superficial circulation, these [skin areas] become irritated mostly by lack of perfect cleanliness. The infectious forces entering are also enabled to do so by the depleting in those particles or effluvia of the blood itself. Which [means that they] attack, then, the mucous membranes of throat, eyes, mouth and nasal passages, but may also be absorbed by the emunctory centers from the groin, under the arm, the knees, the elbow.

"These are the sources, then, these are the manners, then, of the infection, of the infected condition that may arise, whether from contact or from the air.

"As we find, then, this is of a glandular inception, or of a type as indicated where there may be many in a household [exposed to the germ] and only a few affected. [This indicates] that the glands of some are more active than the glands of others."

As a preventive against polio, Cayce's recommendation was the use of a form of iodine developed through independent research aided by study of the Cayce readings. It was not to be taken internally while any other drug was being taken.

As a polio preventive, this iodine preparation was to be used in sponge baths, "for the elders, for the nurse, or for those about [the polio patient] . . . especially around the arms, the groin and such portions of the body. [Use] a spray of a similar 50 percent solution of commercial strength for throat, nasal passages and the like. And the taking of same internally by those that apparently have been exposed to the conditions—one to two minims morning and evening, in periods, and then a rest period, and then take it again . . ."

In 1962, a news report told of a study which seemed to indicate some antipolio properties in the conch, a large sea snail eaten extensively by people in the Bahamas.

According to this report, there had been only fifteen cases of polio in the Bahamas during the preceding ten years. Had the incidence corresponded with the rate of incidence in the United States during that same time, there would have been 177 cases there.

On the island of Bimini, the children begin eating the conch—raw, in salads, fried, in stews, etc.—from the time they stop nursing. On Nassau, the conches are eaten only occasionally. It was on Nassau that most of the fifteen cases of polio occurred.

The report contained the additional information that recent research had indicated certain antipolio qualities in
125

the juice of abalone. Abalone, as well as conches, are of course rich in iodine. Although this is not proof of the accuracy of Cayce's pronouncements on the subject of polio, for there may be other factors involved of which we have no knowledge, we believe it merits further study.

Then there's the case of an eighteen-year-old boy suffering from leukemia, who was given a series of Cayce readings in 1941.

Among the remarks on diet, which according to the readings was of paramount importance in treating this patient, Cayce made an exceptionally interesting statement. "Include as much orange juice as may be easily assimilated by the body; preferably the Florida grown and tree-ripened fruit. This supplies the elements needed."

In an article in *Saturday Review* of June 1, 1968,[1] there is a statement by the author, Solomon Garb, M. D., concerning evidence that a relative shortage of ascorbic acid (Vitamin C) in the bodies of leukemia patients may be the cause of some of the more distressing symptoms of the disease. According to Dr. Garb, recent research indicates that leukemic cells may take up all the available ascorbic acid in the body, leaving so little of it in the plasma and tissues that the patient develops the symptoms of scurvy. Apparently normal doses of ascorbic acid are not enough; Dr. Garb suggests that experimental treatment with massive doses of ascorbic acid might well relieve some of the most distressing symptoms of leukemia. He thinks it might even prolong the victim's life.

Oranges, of course, are rich in Vitamin C.

And then there's the matter of coffee. This was often recommended in the readings to be taken not simply as a drink, but as food.

Said one reading, "For the food value and the proper strengthening, coffee should be taken without either cream or sugar." Said another, "Coffee taken properly is a food; that is, without cream or milk."

In *Rx Health* magazine for February, 1964, there was reported that, as a result of biological analyses, coffee has been shown to contain appreciable amounts of the B vitamin, niacin, as well as small amounts of other B

[1] "Neglected Approaches to Cancer, "SR June 1, 1968

vitamins. It contains, as well, the minerals sodium, calcium, iron and fluorine. Demitasse coffee was said to contain from 45. to 46.5 mg. of niacin per 100 grams of coffee. Further, four cups of dark roast coffee were found to supply from 9.6 to 13.4 mg. of niacin, or enough to provide the minimum daily requirement.

Space does not permit our making more than a rather casual reference to such items, and we have had to limit ourselves to a small sampling of the kinds of information given years ago in the Cayce readings that are being borne out by modern scientific research. In the areas of diet, exercise, and healing techniques much has occurred in recent years to indicate that Cayce's source of information—although presented in an everyday, commonsense manner—was actually highly sophisticated and advanced.

Only now, so many years after the death of Edgar Cayce, do we seem to be on the verge of realizing the potential worth of the material contained in the physical readings. An item in the publication, *A.R.E. News* for September, 1968, indicates that the research program among physicians associated with the Medical and Osteopathic Research Divisions of the Edgar Cayce Foundation is well under way.

States this report, "Work at a clinical research level on epilepsy, multiple sclerosis, schizophrenia, deafness, baldness and a number of other diseases and syndromes has begun to show results which should be interesting and informative. The number of cooperating physicians continues to grow apace."

CHAPTER TEN

TELEPATHY AND/OR CLAIRVOYANCE
AS SHOWN IN THE LIFE READINGS

We have just examined, in some detail, a number of
physical readings given for individuals by Edgar Cayce.
We have illustrated that they were helpful, when there was
cooperation on the part of patient and physician, and we
have shown that they were surprisingly accurate. We do
not have to *assume* they were accurate; in many cases
what the readings had to say about physical conditions
was borne out later by x-rays, blood tests, or other
medically acceptable means. In other words, they were
provable.

Now we move into an area where there can be little
proof of accuracy. As we consider the second major type
of reading given for individuals, that called the life reading, we must do so in the knowledge that there is no way
to substantiate much of what Cayce had to say.

That he was able to describe accurately the personal
characteristics of the subject of his reading is, at least to
some extent, provable. The subject himself, or someone
who knew him, might testify that Cayce had certainly
described the person's attitudes, his talents, or his physical
characteristics, extremely well. But there is the chance
—at least in some cases—that this was a telepathic communication and nothing more.

We could suggest that, although Cayce's physical
readings were astounding enough in their accuracy to
shake even the most ardent skeptic, when he began to talk
of the past lives of an individual and how these affected
his present life, he was way out in left field. But would this
be a reasonable assumption? Would it make sense to say
that Cayce, in one regard, was amazingly clairvoyant, and
in another regard was talking out of his psychic hat?

Would it be reasonable to assume that this humble and
uncomplicated man, this Sunday school teacher, who had
no interest in or knowledge of other than the most orthodox Christian beliefs, *wanted* to receive information

about ancient religions, about reincarnation, and thereby "sell" such ideas to a doubting society? Hardly. For some time after the subject came up in his readings, he tried to deny its validity.

About all we can do, at this stage, is to offer some examples of life readings, and ask that you read them with an open mind. If you are skeptical about such matters, you may well come away from them just as skeptical as ever. If you are undecided about your feelings on the subject of reincarnation, you may still be undecided after you have read some of what Cayce had to say. If you happen to believe in the possibility of reincarnation, you may find some fuel to feed your belief. In any event, we think you'll find these readings highly interesting.

To understand and appreciate Cayce's clairvoyance as it was demonstrated in the life readings, it is necessary to have some knowledge of the basic philosophy behind them. A full treatment of this could well fill its own book, so we will satisfy ourselves, here, with a brief explanation.

Perhaps we should begin with a restatement of the suggestion used to obtain the life readings, which was supplied by Cayce while in trance in 1925, just after reincarnation had been introduced as a subject of the readings:

"You will have before you the body (give name and place of the individual at birth, the name at birth as given) and you will give the relation of this entity and the universe, and the universal forces, giving the conditions that are as personalities latent, and exhibited, in the present life. Also the former appearances in the earth's plane, giving time, place, name and that in that life which built or retarded the development for the entity, giving the abilities of the present entity and that to which it may attain, and how."

This suggestion, said Cayce, would make it possible to know the effect "not only of the present environment, as it has been, as it may be, but the effect of the past experiences and through what sphere these were obtained."

According to Cayce's information, as shown in the readings, God created, of Himself, souls. As he stated in one reading, "The soul is that which the Maker gave to every entity or individual in the beginning. It is seeking the home or place of the Maker."

In another reading, he said, "The soul is an individuality that may grow to be one with, or separate from the Whole."

And in another, "What, then, is a soul? What does it look like? What is its plane of experience or activity? How may ye find one?

"It may not be separated in the material world from its own place of abode in the physical body. The soul looks through the eyes of the body; it feels with the emotions; it develops awareness through the faculties in every sense —and thus adds to its body, just as food has produced a growing physical body."

A soul, according to Cayce, spends many lifetimes on earth, separated by other periods in which it resides in the spirit world, preparing itself for its next return to earth. The periods between "lifetimes" are spent in developing itself, just as it is designed to do when in earthly form, trying to reach the perfection that will make it someday worthy of returning to God.

Each earthly appearance, say the readings, has its gains and its losses. Gains, in terms of spiritual development, advance the soul toward its sought-after perfection. Losses, through succumbing to sins of the flesh, result in debts that must be paid in future earthly appearances. This is the law of karma, or the law of retribution, which Cayce clearly explained in a reading given in 1933.

"Karma is a reaction which may be compared to the reaction within the body when a piece of food is taken into the system.

"The food is translated into a part of the body itself, penetrating to every cell, and influencing the health of the body and mind. Thus it is with a soul when it enters a body for an experience in the earth. The person's thoughts are the food upon which the soul feeds, along with the actions which result from these thoughts.

"These thoughts and actions in turn have been generated by thoughts and actions behind them, and so on back to the birth of the soul.

"When a soul enters a new body, in a new environment, a door is opened leading to an opportunity for building the soul's destiny. Everything which has been previously built,' both good and bad, is contained in that opportunity.

"There is always a way of redemption, but there is no way to dodge responsibilities which the soul has, itself, undertaken. Thus a life is a way of developing, a preparation for the cleansing of the soul, though it may be a hard path at times for the physical consciousness and the physical body.

"Changes come, and some people say luck has intervened. But it is not luck. It is the result of what the soul has done about its opportunities for redemption."

According to the readings, when God created souls, He gave them free will. Thus it is up to each soul, working its way through many appearances in the earth, to develop toward its original objective: to be a fit companion to God. The readings suggest that each soul chooses its time and place to be "born" into a new life on earth, selecting the environment and the company of other souls with which it may best work out its own destiny.

They also suggest that souls tend to incarnate in a kind of group pattern. This accounts for the fact that so many people who had Cayce readings were found to have had previous incarnations with others for whom readings were given. Many of them, particularly those who worked closely with Cayce in the present life, had been associated with him in some way in past incarnations. The majority of people who received readings were found to have had incarnations in one of two general patterns: Atlantis, Egypt, Rome, the Crusades period, and the early colonial American period; or Atlantis, Egypt, Rome, France in the time of Louis XIV, XV or XVI, and the time of the American Civil War. (These, however, were "highlight" incarnations given by Cayce as being most pertinent to the present life; there may have been others which did not affect the present incarnation particularly.)

Because, as we have mentioned, each soul writes its own history upon the akashic records, and retains the memory of all its experiences, it was possible for Cayce, as stated in the readings, to "tune in" and read the history for the person seeking information via Cayce's psychic abilities.

Pamela Winters: A Study in Character

One of the clearest examples of Cayce's ability to describe the personal characteristics and talents of another is seen in the case of Pamela Winters.

At the time of the reading, Pamela was fourteen years old. Thus it is possible that much of the information given in the reading was received telepathically by Cayce, for by that age personal traits are fairly well developed in the individual. Other parts of the reading may not be so easily explained, as we shall see.

We will offer the reading in its entirety, just as it was given on July 22, 1944. However, we will interject into the reading at appropriate points some portions of an A.R.E questionnaire answered by Pamela's mother five years later, concerning her opinion of Cayce's accuracy.

Reading

"Yes, we have the entity here, Pamela Winters. Here we find very unusual abilities and also some very unusual warnings to be given for such a lovely person. [Cayce had never seen her.]

"In the interpretation of the records, these would be first directed to [the parents] who [are responsible for] giving the opportunity for the entity [to develop] its abilities, especially in that field of art which would be designated as place cards, Christmas pictures, season's greetings and that particular nature. These should be the opportunities given the entity. This necessarily would include music, but not music as a means of doing other than attuning or giving expression.

"For the entity of its inner self is very psychic. Do not submerge, but rather encourage all such."

Questionnaire

Pamela's mother indicated that Pamela had no particular interest in art or sketching, "but decided emphasis on self-adornment. She is artistic and luxurious in taste; loves elegance." As to any demonstration of psychic ability or particular interest in music, her mother answered with a question mark.

Reading

"There will be these as warnings, these for those responsible for the entity: a tendency for the body to overeat or to be overindulgent in appetites. Be warned for self, as well as associates of those who take wine or strong drink, for this may easily become a stumbling block for the entity.

"In giving the interpretation of the records for the entity, these opportunities, these privileges and these warnings should be directed more to [the parents.]"

Questionnaire

Mrs. Winters indicated that Pamela had always been inclined to overeat. However, concerning a tendency to be attracted to those who overindulge in liquor, she said that Pamela had married a young man from a family of heavy drinkers, although he seemed to be quite level-headed about the problem. Pamela, said her mother, had always had a strong aversion to liquor.

Reading

"As to the entity, we find Venus, Jupiter, Mars, Saturn, all of these are parts of the entity's consciousness. Thus a very strong-minded individual, but one given to light things; and yet one very capable when talking to individuals, rather than groups or numbers of people.

"Thus those warnings should be: make the self, then embrace opportunities with groups and others. Do apply self in the direction especially of art and music. For these will offer the channels, especially as has been indicated, through which not only the material success may be gained but the interpretation of the physical, the spiritual, the psychic. Don't be afraid to acknowledge that ye see fairies as ye study, for you will nurture these experiences. Don't be afraid to say that you see the gnomes which would hinder people at times. These may be a part of the background for many of the cards, for many of the various sketches which you would make."

Questionnaire

Concerning a tendency to be with individuals, rather than groups, Mrs. Winters indicated that Pamela ". . . prefers one or two people at a time. She's quite critical of people; too discriminating. She is not outward-going!" Pamela, said her mother, "is very strong-minded, but still very much attracted to light topics of conversation and interest."

Reading

"As to the appearances in the earth, these have been quite varied.

"Before this we find the entity was in the land during that period when there were those reconstructions following the period called the American Revolution. Here we find the entity interested in building a home with the beautiful grounds about same.

"In the name then Lila Chapman, the entity gained through the period, for the home to the entity and its family and its children was that which took the greater portion of its time, save the study of the Word which was given place in that home. And yet there came from same those who took too much of the cup, as cheers. This brought disturbances, sorrows. Don't let it occur again. There will be the tendencies for attraction, not only for self, but for those about you. For that ye hate has come upon thee. Don't hate anything in the present."

Questionnaire

Mrs. Winters stated that Pamela had never shown much interest in church or the Bible. However, since childhood she had shown great concern for the care of orphans. Regarding a tendency to want a fine home and grounds, however, "Pamela's main interest, particularly since her marriage, has been in beautifying her home. She has a driving ambition to own, someday, a really elegant place."

Reading

"Before that, we find the entity was in the lands to which the Apostles went when they were driven, because of persecutions, to the Holy Land, and those parts of what is Asia Minor or the old portions and to Persia; and we find the entity, not as a 'hanger-on' but as one who aided the Disciples, who followed through in these directions with John in one portion of the land, and then with the descriptions of Bartholomew. The entity was closely associated with these in singing psalms and in the alms and good deeds for those attracted to same for the material as well as spiritual portion of their lives. In the experience the entity was then known as Ishneth.

"Before that, we find the entity was in 'the city in the hills and the plains' and the entity was among those of the natives attracted by, attracted to, the peoples who came from the Grecian land, but not for any good purpose. Some succeeded in undermining peoples. Most did not, but became believers themselves. The entity was among those attracted for their beauty, for their grace and most of all for their cleanliness. For cleanliness is next to Godliness. For he who is pure as an individual should be pure in body, as clean in body also.

"In the experience the entity learned much of the mystical, not any of the Persian, but those activities in 'the city in the hills,' which aided individuals in the artistic phases of Grecian culture and lore. Thus the interest in the body beautiful, the interest in nature and nature's dwellers in air, as well as from flowers, roses, clouds, trees, water, sounds and all of these which come from nature itself. The name then was Pleghen."

Questionnaire

Now we come to a most striking parallel between Pamela as seen by Cayce in his reading and Pamela as seen by her mother. Said Mrs. Winters, "Pamela is decidedly a clean person, even from babyhood. She never even looks slightly soiled. If a bug came upon her clothes or bedcovers, she had to immediately change them. She always smells delicious.

"In a romantic and sensual way, she appreciates beauty. However, as of this stage in her life, she has shown no particular interest in Grecian culture and lore, or in the mystical."

Reading

"Before that, we find the entity was in the Egyptian land when there were those who were a portion of that development for Ra Ta [Edgar Cayce was Ra Ta, a priest in Egypt, in an early incarnation] in bringing perfected

135

children into the earth. The entity was among those who were of that individual's activity and yet brought into the service in the Temple of Sacrifice and the Temple Beautiful the arts which first were expressed in colored flowers upon the linen of the day, and those which made for beauty among the peoples in the homes, as a means for instruction in urging the emotional forces of body, and life-building. The name then was Itcar."

Questionnaire

Mrs. Winters was asked the question, "Is Pamela particularly susceptible or responsive to the opposite sex; or does she have decided views on relationships in home and marriage?"

She replied, "Pamela has decided views on this. She's quite opinionated, and was critical of most boys who were attracted to her because of her good looks. She is repulsed by drinking, petting, dirty jokes, even smoking. She decided at fifteen that she would marry the boy she just married last June, when she was eighteen."

Concerning an interest in flowered linens, and in interior decorating, Pamela's mother replied, "She has a great appreciation of flowers and soft materials such as angora sweaters and silk underwear. She loves perfumes. She enjoys making her home as beautiful as possible."

Reading

Among the questions asked of Cayce at the end of the main portion of the reading were some concerning relationships between Pamela and her present family in previous incarnations, and the influence of this on their present lives together.

Cayce indicated that Pamela had been associated with both parents, and that their readings should be compared to Pamela's. "Parallel with the application of each or the activities in varied experiences. These ye will draw the better in the Egyptian experience."

Concerning Pamela's brother, the two had been associated in two previous incarnations: in Egypt and Persia.

However, concerning Pamela's sister, Cayce said, "You won't get along so well . . . though you love her. You were not associated."

Questionnaire

Mrs. Winters indicated that Pamela and her brother had always been congenial, though their interests were quite different. When asked if Pamela and her sister didn't get along, she replied, "They don't get along at all. Pamela can't stand her sister; the two are direct opposites."

Comments

Cayce seems to have described Pamela quite well, considering her mother's response to the questionnaire. We do not have recent reports, and can only conjecture about the possible development of such matters as an interest in the mystical, which Cayce indicated would be strong influences in this life.

It is important to remember that Cayce's readings were in no way fortune telling, or predictions of what would happen. Their purpose was to guide the individual in making the most of his life, in light of past experiences as well as present surroundings and urges. The person's own free will, and how it was applied, would determine the worth of his lifetime.

If there is one strong point that comes out of Pamela Winters' reading, it is the great influence of past lives in making her the kind of person she was at the time of the reading, or is today.

Such possibilities add all sorts of complexities to our struggle to understand human nature. No wonder a psychiatrist friend of mine, who is dead-set against the idea of reincarnation, said to me recently, "Don't bug me with all this stuff about past lives. Don't you think I have enough to keep me busy, just trying to figure out all the crazy things people do from the time of their birth? If I ever have to start going back into past lives to figure out a human personality, I'll close up shop and take up basket weaving!"

And Always, the Music

Admittedly, mental telepathy might well account for Cayce's accuracy in describing Pamela Winters. She was, after all, fourteen years old at the time of her reading.

But we wonder: could telepathy alone explain such accuracy in the case of Jay Clement? His reading was given in August, 1944, when Jay was ten weeks old.

Cayce began the reading with the type of advice he frequently offered parents of young subjects. "In giving the interpretations of the records as we find them here, there is much to be chosen from. Yet, as to the developing personality of this entity, much will depend upon the guiding of same through the formative experiences in this particular sojourn."

According to the reading, Jay was an unusual entity who had once lived on the lost continent of Atlantis. In his present life, said Cayce, Jay was "one gifted, as will be indicated in the unfolding of the abilities of the body in that called the higher arts, especially of the use of the voice. All of its abilities as a composer, as a singer, should be those things to which those responsible in the present should direct this entity. For this entity was among those who first began to attempt to make music, especially American music."

The reading explained that in the incarnation preceding this one, Jay had been a musician. "These activities should be studied, not merely for meeting the problems as to the character of voice, of music, but to give the entity the advantage especially of piano and stringed instruments of every nature. For the voice will be noteworthy and such as to make a great contribution to true American music." Since he was a highly developed soul, having been once an Atlantean, Jay's parents were warned not to attempt to evade his questions, or to attempt to deceive him, "or you may make a singer on the street, and not a good one at that!"

Said Cayce, "There will be found, as with every true musician or every true artist, one with a great deal of imagination. Do not stop or confuse the entity in the imagination. Not so much as ever discouraging, but do not encourage to that point that it becomes solely imagination for the exaltation of its own ego. The entity will be found to be one quite sensitive, or a psychic of no mean ability." [There are reports from the parents indicating a number of childhood psychic experiences had by this boy.]

The reading stated that, prior to the appearance as the musician, Jay had been "in that land now known as the

Holy Land, during the days when the Master walked in the earth, and during those periods when there was the establishing of churches or groups for the propagation and dissemination of the tenets and truths which were parts of the activity during those periods. The entity, young in years, was among the children in those groups at the feeding of the five thousand. Hence you will always find the entity ready to eat when it is time to eat, and he will expect it to be there, no matter where it comes from!" ["How very true!" reported Jay's parents some years later.]

"This is innate, for—created from that which was a friend's little lunch for the multitudes—why shouldn't a divine Father supply those worthy, and unworthy as well?"

During that appearance on earth, said Cayce, the entity had become a singer in the various churches throughout the land. "For the entity journeyed with Luke and Paul, Paul and Silas, Paul and Barnabas, and thus came in contact with those in many portions of the land; as a psalm-singer of real help, then, to all of the churches.

"Hence psychic experiences, the abilities to speak, the desire to go to Sunday school (and you had better go with him, not send him!) will bring activities in the experience of the entity."

There had been, said the reading, an even earlier appearance in the Holy Land. Again, he had been a psalmist, and had "led in the praises of all the leaders and those who held close to a worship of the holy influences in man's activities.

"In the present the entity will find, then, that groups, crowds, throngs, will be those things which will tend to direct, to aid or deter from the fulfilling, and yet to have the feel of the brother man; for freedom *is* America."

Prior to that appearance, the entity had been in Egypt, "among those who were trained in the Temple Beautiful, as a teacher or lecturer for those of the land of Saad, as well as the Gobi land. Thus we will find in the present the entity will be particularly interested in things oriental, especially Chinese, or the Gobi or parts of the East Indian land."

In the Egyptian experience, he had served "in the ca-

139

pacity of an emissary, as would be termed today, or a representative in other lands. Hence the present interest, as should and will be, in things national and international."

Before the Egyptian experience, said Cayce, the entity had been "in the Atlantean land when there were those disturbances which arose before the second breaking up of the land. This brought a period of trial for the entity. . . . The entity was a prince in the land. . . ."

Bear in mind that Edgar Cayce obtained this information, by his own description as given in the readings, through attuning his unconscious mind with that of another; in this case, that of a ten-weeks-old baby boy!

When the child was four years old, his mother reported that already there were strong indications of an interest in music.

In 1956, when Jay was eleven years old, his mother again wrote to A.R.E. to report his progress. "He has composed about five songs, one of which I feel is very good. He doesn't do so well in school, probably because he daydreams so much. His teacher told me there are times when he will look right at her and she knows he isn't hearing a word she is saying, that he is somewhere away off.

"One day he was working on his arithmetic and stopped in the middle of it. I asked him, 'Aren't you going to finish your lesson before you stop?' He answered that he was hearing music and wanted to go right to the piano and see if he could play it. His difficulty is mostly, so far, in writing it down. He wants to get a harp. He doesn't like violin music. He had an accordion at one time, but does most of his practicing on the piano. He says, 'Sometimes music comes to my mind and I have to stop whatever I'm doing and go to the piano and play.' "

In 1964, just after Jay's twentieth birthday, his aunt reported, "He's now in his second year at the music college. He is a very fine boy, tall and handsome, quiet and home-loving.

"All through high school he had his own band. One summer they played professionally, carrying their instruments around the countryside in a trailer. Jay played the organ, and was manager of the band. Much of their music is of the rock-and-roll type, which is so popular now.

"This past summer, Jay has been working with his father in the construction business, in order to earn money to help with his college expenses. He definitely shows all the signs of being headed for a musical career. He has a splendid speaking and singing voice.

"He was brought up in the Baptist Sunday school, as his parents were staunch members. He always participated and did not object, as some children do, to attending regularly.

"I do not know about his interest in things oriental, especially Chinese. Of course this might develop later, as he is still quite young. He has a wonderful taste in clothes and dresses elegantly.

"Also, I have not heard of any special interest in things national or international, as the reading mentioned, but I do know that he is a very tolerant and broad-minded individual, and a very gifted one."

That Jay has developed along the lines of his reading, both as a musician and as a human being, is probably due to many things. Not the least of these is the environment into which the reading was given.

Jay's parents had both received life readings, and in another reading had been advised by Cayce to marry. Mrs. Clement indicated their respect for this opportunity by reporting at one time, "My husband is quite an individual and a remarkable person in many ways, and we have had a great deal of happiness in being together. We are so thankful we had our readings to guide us."

It is not surprising, then, that they eagerly sought a reading for their first-born, and followed it with considerable dedication. Certainly it is evident that they encouraged Jay's early interest in music by making training in this field available to him.

But this still does not explain how Cayce knew, in giving a reading for Jay as an infant, that he would, and should, be so strongly inclined toward a career in music. And this is not a matter of training only, for Jay obviously has a natural talent for which all the training in the world cannot compensate.

It also does not explain how Cayce knew about the tendency to daydream—a manifestation of the imagination

141

spoken of in the reading, perhaps?—or the evident love for church, and for his fellow man, which have been shown in reports concerning Jay's development. All this, said Cayce, came of earlier appearances on the earth.

It is difficult to review such a reading, and note how accurate it seems to have been in so many respects, without admitting the possibility that reincarnation is a fact, not a theory.

Sober-Sided Charlie

Charlie Roberts' parents had heard of Edgar Cayce, but saw no particular advantage in obtaining a life reading for their six-year-old son. His aunt, however, requested one for him, and it was given in May, 1944.

Again we have a reading which began with Cayce's advice to the parents. "In giving an interpretation of the records here, much rests with the parent as to how completely the entity may fit itself for its abilities and urges latent and manifested in this experience. These as characteristics will be seen with the entity.

"One always wanting to fix something, no matter what.

"The entity is always inclined to want to make something which would be an improvement. -

"Thus, we will find the entity a scientific genius if the opportunities for self-expression are given full opportunity in this experience.

"Those things which would pertain to the study of mind, as well as that which would be applied in making improvements upon things, either electrically-driven or as to improvements or corrections in collecting of data, collecting of interesting experiences of or with individuals.

"There is the bringing to the entity of a tendency to be rather too much inclined to be sober and sarcastic. And this may not turn out so well unless there is given the entity such opportunities to improve the mind, or to study law as pertaining to conditions or things; not so much as having to do with material happenings as with the arbitrary expression from spiritual attributes of individuals."

In the incarnation just prior to this one, he had been "among those who improved the city or the activities in the place of the entity's [birth]. . . . In the experience the entity gained by aiding in the preparation of things pertaining to mechanical appliances which would be labor-saving to man."

In the earliest incarnation given in the reading, "the entity was in the land now known as the Holy Land when the peoples journeyed from Egypt to the Holy Land. The entity was among those who aided some of the sons or children of Dan to prepare the mechanical things for the carrying of the tables, the altar, candlesticks, and those things which were to be used by other individuals.

"In the experience the entity gained the more, and with the application of self came knowledge and power within self to control influences about the entity."

In the question-and-answer section of the reading, Cayce made the statement, "As has been indicated, the parents should make themselves responsible for the administering to the needs of the entity that which will enable him to become a scientist."

Answering an A.R.E. questionnaire in 1949 concerning Charlie Roberts' reading, the aunt replied: "Although the grandmother and parents have read this reading, they aren't interested. He is being given church training; also music." Charlie, she said, had never seen his reading.

Another questionnaire was answered by the aunt in May, 1952, when Charlie was nearly fifteen years old. Portions of her reply which seem to bear out Cayce's analysis of Charlie's nature are as follows:

"He is a very quiet boy, really too sober-minded. He can fix things, make improvements; but I have not noticed that he goes out of his way to do so. His father and mother are quite active in the Methodist Church, and they take him along with them.

"Charlie told me of an incident regarding some work, where two or three boys had to take turns. His turn came last and was difficult, so he figured out an easy way. The other boys 'jumped' him for not telling them how to go about it the easy way, and he replied, 'I never thought of it until it was my turn.'

"Another incident comes to mind. When he was six years old, he set a rabbit trap, and put a carrot inside for bait. Nothing happened. Later, when his mother inspected the trap, she saw an onion and a carrot, and she asked him about it. He said, 'Well, the rabbit could *smell* the onion, and when he saw the carrot he would investigate; then I would have him.'

"He does not like hard work, and never seems to move until a problem is presented, and then the short-cut solution comes to him. He reads constantly, and seems to be looking for explanations and answers. I have very little opportunity to guide him, since his mother opposes anything that is not orthodox. His father doesn't care much one way or the other whether I talk with him along the lines of his reading. I do think his mother is loosening up some, and as time goes on, I hope to have a chance to direct him according to his life reading.

"I have not yet noticed whether he has inclinations toward 'electrically-driven things or collecting data of interesting experiences of or with individuals,' as was indicated in his reading. At this time, he is interested in astronomy.

"I have never heard him make sarcastic remarks, but I have felt it in his attitude. He is such a quiet boy. However, during the little contact I have had with him, I've noticed that he must be pushed constantly to keep going. He seems to stand aside and watch others, questioning why they are doing things in a particular way. You can only force him so far; he just won't be driven."

We do not have recent reports concerning Charlie's progress since 1952. We would hope that what seems to be a natural inventiveness and an active imagination have been encouraged to develop in the way Cayce indicated, so that he will be able to realize his full potential in this life.

"For Weal—Or Woe"

Loretta Monroe was fifteen days old at the time of her reading. It is a remarkable study in personal characteristics and personal prophecy.

The reading is too long to be used in its entirety here. We will give highlights only, and from time to time will interject various reports based on comments made by those who know her. Loretta is now twenty-nine years old, married, and the mother of three children.

144

"Yes, we have the records here of that entity now called Loretta Monroe.

"In giving the interpretations of the records as we find them here, these are chosen with the desire to be a helpful experience for the entity, as well as a helpful influence in the experience of those who will have the guiding of the formative years of the entity in this present earth plane.

"For, without the proper directions—from the experience in the sojourns (and these being many)—the emotions may influence the entity to such an extent as to become a woe in this present sojourn.

"These, then, are chosen with that purpose of making those who have the care of the entity *aware* of those inclinations, those emotions which will become manifested, especially in the formative years.

"In the composite of the latent or astrological urges, and the material sojourns, we find these as influences that will be manifest.

"One that has a temper of its own. While not stubborn—for it can be easily reasoned with—it must have a *positive* answer for every question, and not, 'Don't—because I say so!'

"One that will be beautiful in body, in figure, in the material sense. Do not allow this to become a vain experience for the entity, but keep the mind and body busy in the developing years in constructive ways and thinking.

"And let the life of each about the entity be particularly consistent with the advice that is given."

Reports

Said the mother, in a report given when Loretta was in her early teens, "She's always been just one step short of stubborn. Sometimes, when I was busy with the other children, I'd nearly be driven out of my mind with her need to know *why* something was so. She'd just stand there and stamp her little foot until I stopped what I was doing and explained. It wasn't a matter of demanding attention, per se, but simply that it was extremely important for her to have the whole answer, right now!"

Loretta Monroe is strikingly beautiful. It is quite interesting that Edgar Cayce would know this when Loretta was only fifteen days old.

The urgent warnings not to spoil the child seem directed toward the entire family. Loretta was the first grandchild, and there were many doting aunts, uncles and cousins around who would have been all too willing to spoil her beyond redemption. Cayce's heavy emphasis on this point seems to indicate that in some way he was aware of this special danger.

Reading

"From the astrological aspects, we will find that blue in the clothing, and especially in stones of every nature, should be part of the apparel for the entity; for it will bring not only the vibrations of healing for the entity but a pleasant and a beautiful reaction to the mental efficiencies of the body.

"As to astrological sojourns, we find Venus, Mercury, Uranus, Saturn and Mars as the ruling factors.

"Hence the body-beautiful will ever be as an influence either for weal or woe, as has been indicated, dependent upon that direction given in its formative years.

"From the Mercurian influence we will find that the entity will be quick at all forms of mental grasping in the spiritual or mental or any form of mental exercise, whether it be in economics or in mathematics or any other form.

"Hence those injunctions as to *consistency* in speech and activity of those about the entity in its formative periods."

Reports

Loretta Monroe has always been spiritually aware, and even as a small child gave much evidence that she felt the presence of a living God. Once, when she was about four years old, her mother looked out the window to see Loretta, playing beneath a large tree in the yard, suddenly stop and kneel in prayer. Afterwards, when asked about this, she said, "I was asking God to send me a baby brother." Eight months later, her brother was born.

She was a bright, quick student, and scored extremely

high in her intelligence tests. She had some poetry published in a scholastic magazine at the age of eight.

Reading

"In the Uranian influence we will find the extremes, as to moods that may arise, rather than its activity in the varied fields or spheres of meanings to the entity.

"And, as indicated, there needs to be cultivated the spiritual aptitudes; not by rote or writ, but by reasoning as to the influences wrought within the experience of the entity.

"In Saturn we find changes, that may be very much according to the aptitudes from the Uranian forces. For, much of *material* benefits will be a part of the entity's experience. Let this not spoil the entity in its formative years, in disregarding values of every nature in its experience.

"Most everyone who meets or is acquainted with the entity, because of these very influences, will wield an influence; and will *want* to give - give - give - give to the entity.

"Thus, none need ever fear as to the material benefits for the entity; but there will need to be the directing as to the evaluations of such in its experience, in its formative years.

"There will be great attractions for the entity to the opposite sex. Hence there would be the warning that there be not an early marriage for the entity, for this would bring the Saturn as well as the Uranian influences in those activities through the Venus forces—which will occur in the experience through its seventeenth to eighteenth year of experience in this sojourn."

Reports

Note again the heavy emphasis on the need for guarding against spoiling the child. Her mother has reported that this was always a problem, within such a large, loving family.

One of the most striking statements in this portion of the reading has to do with the danger of an early marriage, during the entity's seventeenth to eighteenth year. At the age of seventeen, Loretta eloped with a boy from her home town. The marriage was annulled soon afterwards.

She married again a few years later, to a fine young man who has worked a small business into quite a large one. His attitude certainly matches the part of the reading that indicated that everyone would want to give - give - give to Loretta; he works extremely long, hard hours to provide her with every possible comfort.

Reading

In discussing her previous incarnations, Cayce stated that the one just prior to the present was as a well-known temperance leader who also did much work for underprivileged children. From this experience, said Cayce, "even in its early years there will be the desire to take sides with all of the little colored children, as well as all the little poor children about the entity; not caring for others."

Earlier incarnations had been in France, where she had been martyred; in the Holy Land, "during those periods when the Master walked the earth"; in Persia as a nurse; in Egypt, in the Temple Beautiful. In this experience, said Cayce, "The entity brought much of that which aided womankind, all of her sex, in greater activity; as did the entity in the sojourn just before the present bring to her fellows an aid towards freedom of speech, as well as the privilege of owning, holding possessions in the own name.

"As to the abilities of the entity, then:

"Much, as indicated, depends upon the manner in which the early periods of its experience are directed.

"If guided aright, the abilities will manifest to constructive forces. If left, it will depend upon circumstance.

"Make them rather in accordance, then, with grace and mercy—through love, through kindness, through patience —that there may be the full manifestation again of that which may bring freedom to many."

Reports

Loretta's parents, and others who know her, have reported that everything in this reading seems to apply directly to her; that it is remarkably accurate. She has a

148

strong, quick mind, a beautiful body, and a deep concern for the welfare of others—particularly those less fortunate than she.

Her reading indicates that the major accomplishments of her life, if properly directed, will take place during the middle and later years. She is still young, and much remains to be seen as to how well she lives up to her potential.

"She Should Be Called Lilith Ann"

Thus Edgar Cayce began his reading for a two-day-old baby girl in April, 1933. Since her parents did not follow this advice, we will use the name for the purposes of this report.

Cayce explained why he had so named her. "In entering, we shall see that this name has been and is indicated in the entity's development—and the entity's appearance in the earth's plane in the present. For *many* shall be those influenced by the activities of the entity's sojourn through this experience."

Describing her personality as it would develop, he said, "One, then, that will be found to be innately tending, and developing, toward headstrongness; great mental abilities. She will be able—and will have those tendencies when speaking—to argue anything down in another individual; a tendency for the obtaining and retaining of all that comes in the experience of the entity.

"Not that selfishness will prevail, but this must of necessity be one of those things that the training and environ must be warned concerning, that this does not become a fault for this entity, Lilith Ann. . . ."

In her most recent incarnation before the present, said Cayce, Lilith Ann had lived in Plymouth. Her name then had been Ann Lilith Bewton. She had been beautiful, with an excellent mind, and had given "self in the services of those peoples, especially in leading the singing and the music in the spiritual service in that day." She had suffered in body "for the tenets held." This, according to Cayce, would "make in the present experience for those periods when, with a scolding or rebuke, the body will turn within itself but not forget its aim or purpose—and, unless watched, will 'do it anyway!'

149

"After the fifteenth to sixteenth year in the present experience, from the sojourn in Plymouth, there will be those tendencies towards the abilities to direct and lead; for the entity will ever be rather inclined to lead than be led—either by her own sex or others! For she'll make many men step around!"

In an incarnation previous to the one in Plymouth, she had been "in that land known as the Roman, when those peoples were being persecuted for their beliefs in the spiritual lessons that were being given during those periods."

She had been in the court of the rulers and, said Cayce, often had been rebuked by her associates, for she had courted favor and tried to combat the decadence of the court. "Yet," he said, "throughout the experience the entity kept self above those even of its surroundings, and never submitted of self to those indulgences as did many of the associates through the period."

Thus she had gained in that experience with regard to the development of soul. She had lost, somewhat, in that her release from an arranged and disagreeable marriage was achieved through suicide.

"In the present, then, there may be seen in the developing years those periods of sullenness; yet of cheerfulness to carry one's own point," It would be this ability, especially through the latter portion of her present life, which would "bring succor, aid, comfort and cheer to the experience of many."

Prior to the Roman incarnation, she had been in India, had suffered in body, and had been healed. She had dedicated the balance of her life to helping others. (This is interesting in light of what happened to Lilith Ann in her present life, which we will discuss later.) Her name, then, had been Lillila. (This similarity of names throughout various incarnations appears often in the Cayce readings. We cannot account for it.)

She had been in Egypt before that, in the Temple Beautiful. Her activities there had been in connection with music and dancing, and these interests, said Cayce, would be shown to be very strong in her present life.

Before that, she had been "in that period known as the Atlantean, among the sojourners from Atlantis who came to what is now known as Yucatan—and was in the temple

150

worship there." Her name in that incarnation was, again, similar to many of her other ones: it was Lilithe.

From her activities in that experience, said Cayce, would come a strong tendency—and a desirable one—to become a vocational counselor or a teacher in the present life.

There were some interesting cautions in the reading concerning health and bodily safety.

"The greater precautions for the health, the welfare of the entity, and warnings, will come during—or should be given for—those periods in October and November of the first four years of sojourn in this experience. And especially for those things that interfere with the sensory system, in the throat and ears. In those periods, then, there should be precautions as to disease that would disturb these portions of the system particularly."

It could, of course, be mere coincidence that just after her fifth birthday, Lilith Ann had her tonsils and adenoids removed.

"And there should be precautions also in the fifth and seventh years, in December and January, as to fire. For, in those periods will the entity be passing through the fiery sign for the entity."

We have no record of any incident concerning fire during this period—or any other, for that matter.

"As to the next influence, or those periods when there come those changes in the physical and developing periods, or in the fourteenth to the fifteenth year . . . will be those periods when there may be seen the greater influence upon the entity from astrological viewpoint—in Uranus. Hence the period of the greater anxiety by or from those upon whom the training of this entity depends."

Again, it could be mere coincidence that, at the age of fourteen, a tremendous change entered the life of Lilith Ann. She contracted polio at that age, and has spent all the years since her recovery in a wheelchair.

Reports from her grandmother indicate a rather remarkable progress, despite the restrictions imposed by Lilith Ann's paralysis. (We should add that there seems to have been no particular emphasis placed on the importance of the reading in guiding her development. Her grandmother had requested it, and the parents seem to have had little interest in it.)

In October, 1947, the grandmother wrote to A.R.E., stating, "Lilith Ann is progressing from her attack of polio last April, but it is very slow. . . ."

In December of the same year, she wrote, "Lilith Ann has not recovered from the polio yet. She hopes to get to Georgia, to Roosevelt's place, in a short time. . . ."

Lilith Ann's aunt wrote to A.R.E. in July, 1951. "Perhaps it would interest you to know that she is intending to teach disabled people handicrafts after she leaves school, where she is majoring in art. She is in a wheelchair. If I remember rightly, it said in her reading that she might go in for vocational guidance or teaching, and I think her work will be very similar to that. . . ."

There are several additional reports on file, all from the grandmother. In December, 1951, she wrote, "Lilith Ann carries herself with great courage and is studying hard in junior college. . . ."

In July, 1952, she reported, "Lilith Ann graduated from junior college and is full of courage. She was on the honor roll, and expects to go on to regular college, if they can make arrangements. . . ."

In March, 1955, she wrote, "Lilith Ann graduated from college with high honors and is teaching incapacitated children. . . ."

In January, 1957, the grandmother reported that, although still confined to a wheelchair, Lilith Ann had been married the previous June. "He must be a nice man, for he carried her into church. . . ."

In March, 1957, a letter from the grandmother indicated that, although still in a wheelchair, Lilith Ann was expecting a baby in April.

And she reported in April, 1958, "Lilith Ann expects her second baby shortly. Polio is a strange sickness. It affects the nerves of the limbs, but the organs are healthy. Of course, the baby will have a Caesarean birth . . ."

There seems to be no doubt that, in spite of physical hardships, Lilith Ann is fulfilling the promise indicated in her life reading. In two previous incarnations, according to her reading, she had "suffered in body," but had overcome her suffering and devoted her life to helping others.

She has done the same in her present life. Certainly we cannot doubt that she possesses high mental abilities, and has put them to good and unselfish purposes.

In considering the reading, and noting its accuracy as shown in the development of Lilith Ann, it seems almost incredible that it was given when she was only two days old.

The Important Formative Years

Robert Allison's life reading was given when he was nine months old. We will print it in its entirety, inserting, at appropriate points, various reports we have concerning him.

Reading

"Yes, we have the records here of that entity now known as Robert Allison.

"Here we have rather an exceptional entity—because of preparations in the minds and hearts of the parents, especially of that entity carrying and caring for this entity through those periods of gestation.

"An exceptional musician, especially piano. If the opportunity is given here, we may have to the musical world of America what Sir Joshua Reynolds [the portrait painter] was in his field—for it is the same entity."

Reports

Robert's mother has reported that only a few weeks after conceiving him, she went into a church and prayed that her child would love music, especially the piano. There are no musicians in the family. This prayer was held throughout her pregnancy, and may account for Cayce's statement in the second paragraph of the reading.

Reading

"In giving the interpretations of the records as we find them here, we choose these with the desire especially that these may prove helpful to those responsible for the entity during the formative years of its experience in this particular sojourn.

"As we find, these are the urges:

"One who will be subtle in its manner of approach to its

153

own individual problems, thinking long and deep, and usually having its own way. Then, unless there is some thought or care taken in meeting these, we will find that the entity may become inclined toward being over-headstrong; yet we will find a gentleness, a seriousness, though periods when there will be tendencies towards recklessness.

"These are the warnings, then, that should be considered in meeting these. Knowing what to look for as the mind unfolds for the entity, we will be capable of meeting these and of directing the entity.

"Do give the opportunity for music. Let the entity listen to and be guided by, not that character of music that is of the passing fancy but that which builds harmony, that which builds the bridge between the sublime and the finite—or from the infinite to the finite mind. Cultivate these more often in the body-mind as it unfolds. Thus we will find less and less of the tendency for headstrongness.

"But there will be periods of temper. We find that this can be controlled, for as indicated, this is an unusual entity in those fields of activity suggested."

Reports

"True," said the mother when questioned about Robert's personal characteristics several years after the reading was given. "In every respect, Cayce was 100 percent correct. My boy is a mixture of seriousness, stubbornness, high temper and at the same time a great deal of gentleness. It is a strong mixture that has puzzled and confused me at times."

Reading

"Astrologically, we find urges from Venus, Mercury, Mars, Jupiter and Uranus. These are tempered ever by the unusual or the extremes that will be found in activities.

"From Venus we find urges related to the beautiful; inclined towards spiritual or sacred music. These backgrounds will be an excellent basis for the entity's development and unfoldment.

"As soon as it is practical for the entity to sit close to a musical instrument, especially a piano, begin to practice on same. Let it be a part of the entity's experience for the

154

next eighteen years to practice some time during each day.

"Thus there will be brought the realms of the infinite through and to those who seek to know much of the spiritual in the experiences in the earth."

Reports

Here we have a case of a reading's being a mixed blessing. The mother, although grateful for the opportunity to understand her boy's moods and talents as shown in the reading, has been in some ways haunted by it.

She set up a schedule of piano lessons beginning at the age of seven, and Robert was excited and pleased about this. But they lived in a small town, where few if any of the boys his age studied music. Upon learning about Robert's lessons, his friends teased him, and he stubbornly refused to go ahead with them. From time to time throughout his childhood, his mother attempted to coax him to the piano. Although she would see him hanging around it, fiddling with the keys when he wasn't aware anyone was watching, he'd turn away from it as soon as the subject of lessons was broached.

He did play drums in his school band. But when he was told that, in order to continue, he would have to learn to read music, he adamantly refused.

By this time, he was aware that a Cayce reading had been given for him. His mother, afraid of overemphasizing the importance of the reading to Robert's development, tried to let him gradually drift toward music as a natural expression.

Reading

"Before this [incarnation], as indicated, the entity was an artist. Thus the harmony, the desire ever in that experience to be the musician—as it was in part during that sojourn; giving the greater expression, of course, in composition. This will be a portion of the expression in the present—the composition of sacred music and classic music. For the entity may write that which will mean from this period on as much as that by Sir Joshua Reynolds in regard to the Holy Family.

"Before that, the entity was in the Holy Land when there were those activities in which there were the gatherings of those who sought to carry on the activities of the Master.

"The entity was among those who added music to the service that brought the oneness of mind, not only in song but in the music of the instrument. For then the stringed instruments were used, but the piano—which should be used in the present—is by nature a stringed instrument.

"The entity then added to that hope, that faith, that understanding, by keeping that touch which would span the varied realms of thought.

"The name then was Sylvesta.

"Before that, the entity was in the Egyptian land during those periods when there were the preparations for greater service of individuals in specific activities.

"The entity then especially through the Temple Beautiful brought to others its activities in music—in the two, three, four, five-stringed instruments.

"The name then was Celeresbestuen."

Reports

Despite his many protestations, Robert seems to love music. Two years ago, he bought a guitar. He plucks at it often, but refuses to learn to play it properly. He enjoys listening to music of all types, particularly that played on the piano and the sitar, and has a large record collection.

He has composed songs. A few years ago, a friend wanted to publish one of them, but Robert refused permission for this.

He has just finished serving two years in the Marine Corps. Said a fellow Marine, "He sings beautifully. In the barracks, he sang us to sleep every night."

It should be noted that he did not particularly like military life. However, the serious side of his nature prevailed; he made up his mind that, if he had to spend his time in this manner, he'd make a good job of it. He finished boot camp second in his class, topped only by a young man who had spent his childhood in military schools.

Stubbornness and high temper seem to prevail in his nature, just as Cayce indicated would happen if he were not allowed the tempering influence of performing music.

"As to the abilities of the entity in the present:

"Much will depend upon the formative years, as to what will be the outcome, by the manner in which the trainings begin.

"Do give the entity the opportunity for activities in the direction indicated, for it will mean much to many peoples.

"And keep the entity close in that realm of spiritual understanding."

In the question-and-answer portion of the reading, Cayce was asked, "What, specifically, are the problems he should work out for himself during this particular sojourn on earth?"

Cayce replied, "As just indicated: its stubbornness in having its own way!"

He ended the reading with the statement that has come to haunt this boy's mother for years, for she has not been able to break through the streak of resistance to see it accomplished in her son. "Do have some period each day from now on—from now—for eighteen years—to practice the music!"

Reports

Robert, with military service behind him, has entered college and is studying architectural engineering. This seems to be another of his strong talents. A family friend, reporting to A.R.E several years ago, stated, "Robert is extremely talented along the lines of mechanical drawing; he can sit down and sketch off anything. Guess that's the trait he inherited from his great grandfather, who was a contractor." (Or is it, we can't help but wonder, a talent brought forward from his former incarnation as an artist?)

That Robert is headstrong there can be no doubt; that he is stubborn almost to a fault cannot be denied. But this is only one side of his nature.

On the positive side, he has a quick, retentive mind, a thirst for knowledge, a charming personality, and an extremely handsome and healthy body. There is no question that he has musical talent, and that one day it may be put to use. It will happen when Robert loses the mistaken impression that his reading, and his mother, were trying to *force* him to be a musician and composer, and when he realizes that he is doing it entirely on his own, simply because he wants to.

CHAPTER ELEVEN

MISSING PERSONS

The locating of missing persons certainly could not be considered Edgar Cayce's long suit. However, he did have some successes, along with a number of misses or near-misses.

The reasons behind this are not altogether clear. There is some indication that Cayce did not feel his psychic abilities should be used for such purposes; that he felt the emphasis of his work should be concentrated in the area of physical problems, or in offering mental and spiritual guidance. He demonstrated this once, when turning down a request from a doctor to locate a friend's missing husband. Cayce's refusal was polite but firm. "We have been advised through the information not to have anything to do with such cases. I am sorry, but I cannot help you."

Often, when he did accede to such requests, he suffered emotionally and physically as a result. Once he was asked to locate a young boy who apparently had been kidnapped from his New York City home early in April, 1938. The reading offered not so much a solution to the case as a question: should Cayce's abilities be used in this way?

As a partial answer to this question, Cayce added, "This is not a condition that is out of the ordinary, but the work of a pervert. Hence it becomes all the more a question as to what the decisions are to be in same; all the more questionable to undertake [such a search.]" Following this reading, Cayce was visibly upset and nervous.

His information concerning the boy seems to have been correct, as far as it went. The child's body was found several weeks later, floating in Long Island waters. There were indications that he had suffered a long and cruel captivity, and there were fragments of heavy baling wire wrapped about one arm.

Possibly Cayce's reluctance in this case was caused, at least in part, by the fact that in 1932 he had unsuccessfully tried to locate the Lindbergh baby. At the request of a friend of the Lindbergh family, a series of readings had been given in which seemingly accurate information was furnished. However, what the readings said did not match up with facts brought out at the trial of Bruno Richard Hauptmann. Hauptmann alone was convicted of the crime, whereas the readings indicated that he had not been working alone. We hasten to add that there were enough discrepancies between the readings and the information brought out at the trial to preclude the need for any serious inquiry into the matter.

It should be noted that the Lindberghs, themselves, did not request the readings. There have been many statements in the readings to the effect that such requests were most likely to meet with successful answers if there was a close relationship between the person sought and the person seeking.

There was a case in 1939 in which Cayce did try to locate a missing sixteen-year-old boy. The boy had disappeared from his home in an eastern city on July 8 of that year. The reading was given on November 25, 1939. Cayce said, "Yes, we have the circumstances and those conditions and anxieties that are manifested here with the mother. These are not altogether pleasant surroundings or pleasant conditions. . . . In the coming months, or in August [1940] there will be the full knowledge and the return of the body to the mother. . . ." (It should be noted that Cayce's use of the word "body" was usual in referring to an individual, and in no way should be considered synonymous with "corpse.")

A family friend located the boy in Los Angeles in July, 1940. The parents, who had initiated the request for the reading, went there and brought their son home. However, they would supply no information whatsoever concerning the details of the case.

The Strange Disappearance of Mark Claypool

Cayce, in trying to locate missing persons, often appears to have been affected by a peculiar sort of block that interfered with the normal performance of his psychic work. No one case better illustrates this than that of Mark Claypool.

Mark was ten years old, severely retarded and a victim of epilepsy. Between July 31, 1929 and January 11, 1932,

Cayce gave thirty-four successful readings for this boy, the last of which furnished a thorough medical picture of the boy's condition, as well as a full progress report on the results of the Cayce-prescribed treatments to date. It advised Mark's admittance to a special school, named in the reading as being best suited to his needs.

Then, around noon on July 12, 1932, Mark's mother telephoned Edgar Cayce's office to request an emergency reading for the purpose of locating her son. He had disappeared just after lunch two days before, while hiking with a number of classmates in the woods at the foot of a mountain. For some reason, the school had waited until just a few minutes before to notify her of Mark's disappearance.

Mrs. Cayce, conducting the reading, began by stating the circumstances as far as they were known. Then she said, "Please trace the movements of this body from Sunday afternoon. July 10, 1932, until the present time, and tell us where he is now and give directions how best to reach him. You will answer questions as they are asked."

Cayce replied, "We do not find him among those on the hike."

"Do you find him at this school or camp during, or earlier, in the day?"

"Do not find him at this camp or school. Find him at lunch, with others."

"Please trace him from the time you locate him. Was Mark at lunch at the camp or school at lunch time?"

"We do not locate him after lunch, here on the grounds, or about the buildings or the camp here."

"Where did he go? Please trace the body from the time you locate him at lunch."

"We do not find him here."

Steadily, Mrs. Cayce continued the inquisition. "Do you find him at the school any time during—"

Cayce interrupted. "At lunch."

"He was there at lunch?"

"He was there at lunch."

"Please follow the body from lunch, tell us where he went."

"We do not find the body."

"What happened to the body?"

161

"We do not find the body."

"Please tell us how we may get information regarding this body through this channel."

"We do not find the body."

"Did Mark leave with the others on the hike to stay overnight about one mile from the school?"

"We find the body at lunch. We do not find him later."

Mrs. Cayce was not yet willing to give up. "Please trace the body's movements from lunch time."

"We do not find the body."

"Where were the movements of the body after he ate lunch?"

"We do not find the body."

"Can you give us any information about Mark Claypool?"

"We do not find the body."

Mrs. Cayce continued rephrasing the questions. Each time, Cayce answered, "We do not find the body." She attempted to lead Cayce into an answer by supplying the material given at the beginning of the reading, the name and address of the school, the conditions leading up to the disappearance. No matter. Cayce would only answer, "We do not find the body."

Finally, she asked, "Can't you trace Mark from the lunch table?"

"Cut off there. We cannot."

"What is meant by 'cut off there'?"

"Can't see him!"

"Can you tell us if anything happened to the body which caused death?"

"We do not find the body."

"Will you please explain to us what prevents you from tracing the body?"

"Something interferes. We do not know."

"In attempting at another time to obtain information regarding Mark Claypool, will you please tell us the best suggestion to give to the body, Edgar Cayce, in order to get information regarding Mark Claypool that we may aid his parents in locating him?"

Normally, Edgar Cayce would have supplied such a suggestion without hesitation. This time, however, he simply said, "We do not find the body."

Obviously, it was hopeless. Mrs. Cayce gave the suggestion for Edgar Cayce to wake up.

Cayce, of course, was terribly disappointed, and planned another attempt at a reading that evening.

Fortunately, it proved unnecessary. About eight o'clock that night the mother called to say that Mark had just been found—on the other side of the mountain, without a stitch of clothing on, all scratched up, dazed and famished. His mental retardation prevented him from telling anything about what had happened to him. He was placed in the hospital, treated for the poison ivy rash that soon developed all over his body, and recovered completely from the effects of his two days in the woods.

It is interesting that a number of additional readings were given for Mark Claypool throughout the next several years, all dealing with his physical condition, and there was never a time when Cayce was unable to get all of the information requested!

The Call That Was Heard

Frank Johnson had once been a wealthy man. The stock market crash in 1929 had taken nearly everything, however, and instead of adapting to his new circumstances, Frank began to misappropriate funds from his firm. By April, 1934, he was in so deep that he simply gave up and dropped out of sight. A note mailed from a city several hundred miles from his home notified the family of what he had done, and indicated that he intended to commit suicide.

His daughter contacted Cayce's office immediately and requested help. There followed a remarkable series of readings in which Cayce several times indicated that he knew Frank's whereabouts, but refused to let the family know where to contact him!

Cayce's concern, it seems, was not only for Frank's safety; there was also the attitude of his family to consider. Should Frank Johnson return home, the story of his embezzlement would most surely become public knowledge. Would the family be able to survive the embarrassment this would cause and continue to love and respect him?

Cayce's readings indicate a three-way purpose: to reach

out and guide Frank Johnson's steps toward home; to reassure the family that he was alive; and to prepare them for Johnson's return. They form a day-to-day drama, and we will give the highlights as they developed.

The first reading was given on April 19, 1934. It began with a statement of the circumstances, as far as they were known, as well as one possible address where Frank might be located. Cayce was asked "to give the family all the necessary instructions and advice as to how they can get to him, if possible, and just what they should do."

Cayce said, "Yes, we have those conditions that confront those of the household, the Johnson family."

The message in this reading was for the family. The overriding theme was, "Would we be forgiven, we must forgive." When asked if Frank Johnson was still alive, Cayce replied, "This should be sought, just now."

A reading given the following day echoed the "forgiveness" theme, and furnished a prayer to be used by the family. Cayce was asked if the family was doing all that it could do, and should do, at that time. He replied, "Doing well. Keep the faith. Pray the prayer, and mean it, and live it, as is given."

He answered a question concerning whether Frank Johnson had assumed a different name, "No. Is he alive, or has he passed on? Let that tell thee that would come to pass, but in His name. *His* desire prevents that which might be given in yes or no; for, he *lives*—ever."

Later that same day, another reading was given in which Cayce indicated that Frank Johnson was "still in the living—still among those that may be reasoned with, in the realm of material understanding." Otherwise, all the information given was of a spiritual nature, directed to the family—although some of it was directed to Frank Johnson.

A few more readings followed, similar to this one. Then, on April 23, Cayce was given this suggestion for a reading: "In appreciation of the help that has been given the soul of Frank Johnson through this channel, we ask that it be continued. And whatever information we or the Johnson family should have, you will give it."

For five minutes Cayce spoke in an undertone so low that nothing could be understood, with the exception of one word uttered toward the end: Philadelphia.

Then, as if speaking directly to Frank Johnson, Cayce said, "The conditions are clearing in thine own consciousness. Then, act on the impulses that prompt thee to make a more determined effort in trusting in *His* promises that what is asked in His name, *believing,* that ye may have, that the Father may be glorified in Him and He in thee." The balance of the reading also seemed directed to Frank Johnson, and was along the same lines.

On April 24, at the end of a reading which had been devoted to spiritual guidance for Frank Johnson in finding his way back to mental health, Cayce said in an undertone, just before waking, "His cough is bad."

The reading suggestion on April 25 indicates that the family had decided to trust in Cayce's ability to follow Johnson's progress and not make a concerted effort to find him. It stated, "In appreciation of the help that has been given the soul of Frank Johnson through this channel, we ask that it be continued and urge him to have faith in his desire for his home. If this condition has reached the point that the entity is not responsible for his physical actions, you will tell us if information may be given those of his family assuming the responsibility as to how to locate him at once."

Cayce stated, "To be sure, further along the way has the body gone physically." The balance of the reading indicated that there was no need for the family to try to locate Johnson at this time.

The reading given the next day was quite dramatic. Cayce opened with the statement, "We don't contact the body!"

Then he began to speak with unusual urgency. "He will come! He will come! He will come! He will come! He will come! He WILL come!

"Let not those things hinder thee! Come! These all may be met in a much more satisfactory manner than has been felt!

"You have seen the way out! COME! Come! You WILL come! You will let those know, and keep that promise to self that you will let them know! Let them know!"

After a long pause, Cayce added, "We do not get the location of the body. It *is* alive—the body.

165

"He WILL come! He WILL come!"

He paused again, and then said, "We are through."

Afterwards, Cayce said that during the reading he had seen woods and water, and that the night before, he had dreamed that Frank Johnson had returned to his home.

Two days later, Cayce began his reading by saying, "We are pressed too tight! We will release through here." He went through a breathing exercise, and then made a surprising statement.

"Yes. As we find, there has been a communication pencilled by Frank Johnson to the family. This should be received very soon—present day or Monday." [The note was received by the family the following day. It indicated that Frank Johnson was alive, but furnished no information concerning his whereabouts or whether or not he intended to return home.]

On April 29, Cayce was asked to "give that which will be of the most help at this time to all concerned, in a material, mental and spiritual way."

He said, "Yes. Yes. We see—we see—oh, where is it? We see the body!" He then gave some spiritual advice.

Later in the same reading he said, "About the body is—what? What is this? What IS this? What IS this? *Where* is it?"

Again there was spiritual advice. Then Cayce said, "*Where* is this? Where is this? What is this about the body that hinders so? That surrounds in such a maze that keeps aid from coming?

"When thou hast chosen those things that block the way for the greatness of the spirit of light to enter, thou makest the way hard even for those that would do thee good. Thou shuttest them out of thine companionship. Thou cuttest them off from being that help and aid that makes for the light that would guide thee.

"This backs away!

"Rise! Make known unto the Lord what thou wouldst do. The mind will clear in Him . . .

"Where is this? *Where?* . . . Still in body!"

A number of readings followed this one, all of which were devoted to aiding the mental health of Frank Johnson. In one of them, on May 3, Cayce said, "Lot of water about the body this morning!" In another, on May 10, he

166

said, "Very much in the open now, and much better is the environ and surrounding." (Following this reading, although all the material in it was of a spiritual nature and not out of the ordinary—for a Cayce reading, that is—Cayce had a strange experience. When he awoke from the reading, he said he felt marvelous, and remarked that he had been having such a good time, he didn't want to come back. Mrs. Cayce, he said, had interrupted him by waking him up; and he couldn't remember what it was he had been doing.)

In a reading on May 11, Cayce again spoke as if directly to Frank Johnson, "More and more do you find the desire in self to make self and self's own activities known to those that long and earnestly seek to know that thou hast chosen in thine weakness and in thine strength in Him to do. . . ."

On the next day, Cayce remarked, "Everything much lighter about the body, about the activities of the soul in the present." It seems, then, that Frank Johnson was indeed breaking through the emotional problems that had so beset him!

Cayce opened the next reading, on May 14, with the statement, "Quite a lot of green about the body; more spirituality coming into the understanding of the self, as to those things that disturb and have disturbed the body in the days just passed . . ." (Green, as you will recall from the chapter on auras, is the healing color. From Cayce's statement we may gather that he was referring to improvement in Johnson's mental state, rather than to his physical surroundings.)

And at the end of the following reading, on May 16, Cayce listened to the suggestion to awaken, except that he did not wait for the final statement, "You will wake up." Instead, he said, "Jesus of Nazareth passeth by. Let Him fill thine heart with the hopes of those promises that are indeed thine, wilt thou but apply. Trust ye in the Lord."

When he was awake, Cayce said that he had seen "the Master walking down a road toward us—*all* of us, expectant, waiting for Him to come—and He was smiling."

A few more readings followed in which Cayce again seemed to be urging Frank Johnson to return home. Then, on May 21, he began a reading by saying, "Yes. The physical body lives. It is among things green, and yet it is the city of those that are called dead." He included in this reading a prayer similar to The Lord's Prayer, but not word-for-word as it is normally used. At the end of the reading, when he was being given the suggestion to awaken, Cayce coughed. He awoke much more slowly than usual, and seemed in a daze for several minutes after apparently waking up.

Still more readings were given in which spiritual advice was offered to Frank Johnson. Then, on June 9, Cayce had just completed giving a physical reading for another individual, and seemed anxious to give one for Frank Johnson. Mrs. Cayce gave him the suggestion for such a reading. At the end of it, he stated, "Much grain about the body—in fields."

The same thing happened a couple of days later, at the end of another physical reading for an individual. Cayce began his reading for Frank Johnson by saying, "More hopeful. More better conditions. Keep the way, for the law of the Lord *is* perfect—converting the soul."

A few days after that, Frank Johnson returned home to a welcoming family. He verified many of the statements in the readings concerning his state of mind at certain times, as well as his surroundings as "seen" by Cayce. For example, he felt sure that Cayce's description, "The body . . . is among things green, and yet it is the city of those that are called dead," referred to the fact that at the time of the reading he had been walking through a cemetery.

When questioned about whether or not he had been conscious of Cayce's telepathic messages to him, urging him to return home, he said that he had not been aware of them as such, although he had felt something "pulling" on him, influencing him in a way he couldn't quite understand.

He managed to make full restitution of the funds he had stolen, and thereafter lived a full and useful life.

Cayce's "Search" for Amelia Earhart

We can make no claims concerning the accuracy of two readings given in 1937 in connection with the disappearance of Amelia Earhart and her navigator, Fred Noonan, during the last leg of their around-the-world flight. No positive statement has ever been made concerning what really happened to them. However, the readings are interesting, and we thought you might like to share some of the highlights.

The first was given on July 5 in answer to a request by a close friend of Amelia.

The reading suggestion was, "You will have before you the request from . . . for information regarding locating Amelia Earhart who, according to radio reports on July 2, 1937, was approximately one hundred miles from Howland Island in the South Pacific Ocean, in her plane. You will locate the plane as of this time and then trace it to its present position, giving specific directions for locating this plane now. You will answer questions regarding this."

Cayce said, "Yes, we have the request, and the anxiety that is manifested in the minds of many at this time. . . .

"As we find, while the conditions are rather serious, by the early morning hours (for it is night there now) there should be the locating from those that are searching in the area.

"This as we find lies in that position opposite from the ordinary for those who lose their way; to the north and to the west of Howland Island, upon the reef that extends from this western portion of the island—about, or in the proximity of less than a hundred miles from the main body of Howland Island; and from Howland Island in that of a westerly, northwesterly, direction."

"What is the present condition of Amelia Earhart and her companion?" he was asked.

"Amelia Earhart in the present is much better, standing the conditions much better than the companion; for the companion has been panicky, and with two these become conditions very much to be reckoned with.

"Not injured bodily so much as from exposure, and the mental condition."

"What happened to the plane? What is the condition of the plane?"

"It is broken up somewhat, but this as we find is more from the attempt in the landing when gas was gone than from anything else; though, to be sure, the winds and the inability to stabilize same has made all very out of order.

169

Not able to proceed even with gas."

Cayce was asked for suggestions in connection with locating Amelia and her companion.

"Serious," he said. "Yet [there are] prospects of locating in this area in the early morning. But it will necessitate light, for there is no way of light for them except flashes—and this is soon giving way."

"Do they have food and water?"

"Mighty little of either.

"Conditions, to be sure, are gradually growing worse all the time. But there should be the rescue with that set in motion, in the early morning of tomorrow—six—which is already beginning, but not fully complete as yet, and more activity is being shown in the right direction now."

At the end of the reading, Cayce remarked that he had seen "myriads of wire netting; some diamond-shaped and others square." This may have been a highly significant statement, as we shall see.

A second reading was given on August 1, 1937, at the request of Amelia's husband, George P. Putnam, through A.R.E. contact of the friend who had requested the first one.

Cayce stated, "As we find, the twenty-first [of July] saw the experience of change in the experience of Amelia Earhart.

"Then, little helpful information may be given, save that: alone she perished.

"Then, this between eighty-nine and ninety miles northwest from her intended destination, or Howland Island.

"Storm—and heat.

"We are through."

Planes had searched the area until July 18. According to Cayce, Amelia had lived three days longer.

Throughout the years since Amelia Earhart and Fred Noonan disappeared, there has been much speculation concerning what might have happened to them. Many stories reporting knowledge of their fate have come to light, but none has survived serious investigation.

None, that is, until a Japanese-born woman living in San Mateo, California, reported to the San Mateo *Times* that she had seen two American flyers, a man and a woman, taken away by guards on Saipan Island in the

Marianas in 1937. This woman, whose name is Josephine Blanco Akiyama, gave accurate descriptions of Amelia and Fred, and furnished a good deal of evidence to support the truth of her story.

Her disclosure was made in May, 1960. It was not the first time she had told her story, but it was the first time it was to be acted upon.

What she had to say did not constitute proof of what had happened to the two flyers, but it was enough to prod a San Francisco radio newsman, Fred Goerner, into beginning an investigation. A joint venture involving Goerner, the Columbia Broadcasting System, the Scripps League of Newspapers, the San Mateo *Times,* and the Associated Press, this intensive investigation spanned the years from 1960 through 1966, and has been fully reported by Goerner in his book, *The Search for Amelia Earhart,* published by Doubleday in 1966.

The conclusions reached at the end of this investigation bear some resemblance to the information contained in the Cayce readings. Neither the investigation, nor the readings, give the final answer to what happened to the two flyers, for as Goerner himself says in summarizing the conclusion, "This is what *probably* happened, based on what we found."

In Goerner's version, Amelia and Fred did not fly directly from Lae, New Guinea toward Howland Island as had been announced in the original flight plan. Instead, they headed north to Truk in the Central Carolines, on an unofficial mission for the United States—that of checking Japanese airfields and fleet-servicing facilities in the Truk complex.

Goerner, an experienced pilot himself, suggests that their Electra, powered by Wasp Senior engines, was capable of speeds ranging from 200 to 220 miles per hour, rather than the 150 miles per hour which had been their top speed during the entire flight. He thinks the higher speed capability may have been deliberately concealed. Thus they would be able to detour over Truk and make good enough time that such a detour wouldn't "show" on the flight records.

When they encountered terrible weather conditions, in the form of strange wind currents—now perfectly calm, now turbulent—they knew they were in trouble. Because Amelia didn't want to be "caught" off to the Northwest of Howland, where she had no business being according to the flight plan, she kept her radio transmissions brief. Clouds obscured the sea for long periods of time, and navigation soon became confused.

Finally, with the gas nearly gone, Amelia, thinking they had overshot Howland, turned the plane around; thus they were actually heading away from their destination. She brought the plane down on a small island which was part of a larger atoll. It seems most probable, says Goerner, that the plane crash-landed in a lagoon at Mili Atoll in the southeastern Marshalls, which was territory mandated to Japan.

According to Goerner's summary of what probably happened, Amelia was not hurt, but Noonan struck his head against some metal in the cabin. His head was cut and he was knocked unconscious. Amelia bound his wounds, and when Noonan regained consciousness, Amelia left the plane to scout the area. Wading ashore, she encountered a number of natives, and managed through sign language to get them to understand that they were to carry Noonan ashore. This accomplished, Amelia then proceeded to send S.O.S. messages from the damaged plane.

Then, said Goerner's summary, on or about July 13, 1937, a Japanese fishing boat picked up Amelia and Fred and carried them either to the Japanese seaplane tender *Kamoi,* or the survey ship *Koshu.* They were taken to Jaluit, then to Kwajalein, and finally to Saipan, Japan's military headquarters in the Pacific. There they were interrogated—cruelly, it is suggested—and there they died; Amelia from dysentery, Noonan beheaded.

On the surface, it may seem that Cayce's readings bore little resemblance to what Goerner has reported in his book as having probably happened.

And yet there are similarities.

The location given in the readings does not seem to jibe. In the first place, there *is* no island 90 to 100 miles northwest of Howland. However, that's where Amelia thought she was when she brought the plane down, and it's possible that Cayce telepathically picked up her conscious thought in this regard; or possibly he accepted the reading suggestion as fact. His statement that they were "in that position opposite from the ordinary for those who lose their way" seems telling, in view of the Goerner statement that they had deliberately gone off course to fly over Truk.

Cayce mentioned high winds and storm. This may well have been a reference to the conditions which had caused them to bring the plane down. He also mentioned lack of gas, which according to the Goerner report was certainly true. Both Cayce and Goerner suggest that the plane was "landed," as opposed to an uncontrolled crash.

In his second reading, Cayce indicated that Amelia had died on the twenty-first of July. This would seem a reasonable date when compared to the Goerner report of their being picked up on July 13 and taken to Saipan for interrogation. Oddly, Cayce, in the second reading, did not mention Noonan's fate—although this might be because Noonan's name was not furnished in the reading suggestion. Cayce also did not give the cause of death in Amelia's case, although his first reading had mentioned "exposure" as contributing to the poor conditions.

The most striking statement, in light of the Goerner report, is the statement at the end of Cayce's first reading, when he indicated that he had seen "myriads of wire netting—some diamond-shaped and others square." This could well refer to the capture and interrogation by the Japanese indicated in Goerner's report. Given on July 5, it could have been a prophetic vision, either symbolic or clairvoyant, concerning their eventual capture. Or perhaps they were captured sooner than July 13, the date fixed by Goerner.

The investigation in which Fred Goerner was involved was a painstaking one, with no arbitrary jumping to conclusions. He told me on the telephone a few weeks ago that it is continuing. So perhaps one day we will have *all* the answers to this thirty-two-year-old mystery.

CHAPTER TWELVE

HISTORICAL DATA
AS SHOWN IN THE EDGAR CAYCE READINGS

There is a wealth of historical data in the Cayce readings. Most often it came as a result of life readings for individuals, wherein historical details concerning previous incarnations reflected the larger history of that entity's time.

Fortunately, on a great many occasions such statements were brought back to the sleeping Cayce for further explanation. Sometimes what he had to say disagreed with accepted knowledge, while at other times his words added to what was already known. In a striking number of cases the data given by Cayce made little sense at the time, only to be proved true in later years by archaeological discoveries or other supporting evidence.

In an earlier chapter, we discussed the case of the reincarnated Salome. Cayce, reading for this woman, indicated that as Salome, she had been present at Jesus' raising of Lazarus from the dead. Years passed before this information, which was at variance with that given in the Gospels, was confirmed through the discovery of ancient written documents.

The range of history found in the readings is astounding. We cannot begin to cover it all within the confines of this chapter, but we can indicate the scope of the material by providing a few examples drawn from readings given by Cayce for various individuals.

In a reading for a four-year-old boy, Cayce said, "Before this, we find the entity was in that land now known as the Arabian . . . then in the name Xertelpes. . . ." (Other portions of the reading make it clear that "Arabian," here, meant Persia—which is now Iran.)

"And the entity was among those that became the first of the crop of judges in the city. . . .

"There still may be found those remains of the entity near where Uhjltd [Cayce, in a previous incarnation] was entombed, in the cave outside of the city that had recently been builded and termed, or called, Shushtar; this to the south and west of that city, in the cave there."

For a forty-two-year-old woman, Cayce said, "Before that we find the entity was in the Chaldean land during those periods when there were the preparations for the peoples called the Jewish or Hebraic to return to their own land, for their establishing again of the activities in their home land.

"The entity may be said to have been the counsellor then to the king, Xerxes.

"The entity then was of the Chaldeans. And there may be found . . . in those excavations—look for same—that rod ye once used in thy divining of the individual purposes during that experience. This will be among those things that will soon be uncovered. It is of ebony and of gold."

For a forty-three-year-old woman, Cayce said, "Before this the entity was in the earth when there were those journeyings from the east to the west—GOLD! In '49 did the entity, with its associates and companions, journey to the western lands.

"Hardships were experienced on the way, yet the entity was among those that did attain, and saw, experienced, was associated in those acts with those that were comparable in their relationships to such conditions: rowdy, drink, spending.

"The name was Etta Tetlow. Records of these may be found in some of the questioned places in portions of California, even in the present."

For a twenty-year-old man, Cayce said, "Before this the entity was in the Norse land, and among those who were the daring, as the sailors; and the entity was Eric, as called through that experience; journeying to or settling in the land of its present nativity [America]."

Cayce was asked, "In the Norse land experiences, how often and in what years did he cross the ocean?"

He replied, "In 1552, 1509 and 1502." (Note that here, as always, Cayce went backwards in giving the dates. This seems to be another indication of his consulting the "record book" mentioned in an earlier chapter—a sort of mental leafing back through its pages.)

In discussing these journeys, he added, "In this country there were the settlements in the northwestern lands; portions even of Montana were reached by the entity—because the entrance then was through the St. Lawrence, through the Lakes."

Asked for proofs that might be found to substantiate this, he replied, "They have just been uncovered by a recent expedition there in Wisconsin . . . Among the knives and stones that were found, one of those was Eric's!"

Even from this small sampling, it is evident that Cayce's sense of geography and history was remarkable. There is also a compelling argument for the accuracy of such statements, it seems to me, in the fact that names furnished for various entities throughout the Cayce files are somehow "right" for the time and place. The name Xertelpes, for instance, given for the young boy mentioned above, fits perfectly in its place in the history of Iran. As was his custom, Cayce paused after reciting the name and carefully spelled it for the benefit of the stenographer recording the reading. (Once again we must remind the reader that Cayce had an extremely limited formal education, and read little outside the Bible during his lifetime.)

There is one more striking quality apparent in the readings. It is possible to go to the Cayce files and pull out any number of readings in which similar incarnations for different individuals are mentioned. Regardless of the number of years that passed between the readings, the facts will be found to coincide, to weave themselves into an intricate whole, with no real contradictions!

The Royal Family

To illustrate this last point, let's examine some readings given by Cayce for several members of the same family.

There are a couple of exceptional circumstances concerning these readings. First, they indicated that some of the entities had been famous during earlier incarnations, whereas the vast majority of Cayce readings were for people whose previous names were not well known. Second, three of these entities were related to each other exactly as before; that is, father, mother and son in one incarnation were again father, mother and son—a rarity among the Cayce readings.

The father, whom we'll call Roger Morrison, received his reading on August 6, 1926. Cayce stated that in his previous incarnation, he had been in France, and had been "the entity known as [King] Louis XVI."

Roger's wife, Sarah, had received her reading about a year earlier on July 15, 1925. Of her earlier incarnation, Cayce said, "We find in that of the Queen who was beheaded, in that of Marie Theresa, or Marie Antoinette, as known in the historic forces. . . ."

In a reading for their son, Charles, on July 23, 1925, Cayce said, "In the appearance before this, we find in that of the entity who was the one to become the King in France, when the father and mother were at that time beheaded. The entity then only gained in the knowledge of the earth's forces, through the things which the entity suffered, for the life at that time was only half a score years plus five."

Sarah Morrison seems to have retained, unconsciously, many "reminders" of the French incarnation. According to notes made in the files by members of the A.R.E. staff who knew her well, we find that Sarah was a woman of "regal bearing. She *is* sort of a 'queen' of a large family, and has the last word on any decision of importance." She was quite tall, and very beautiful.

Another interesting report on her states, "When traveling by train, she would never go from one car to another, for she said she could not bear the sound of the rumbling wheels. Could this be a throwback to the ride over cobblestones to her death?"

Sarah had a great love for beautiful and luxurious things. She was an accomplished painter, and collected fine furniture, old silver and linens. "When she died," says another note in the file, "she left trunks of elaborately embroidered linens. All her life, since a very young girl, she never sat down even for a few minutes without picking up her embroidery." (This could well be an influence brought forward not only from the French, but from a much earlier incarnation in Egypt, of which Cayce said, "The entity then giving much to the people, and the desire to preserve relics, old and new, the desire to preserve the best for the worship of every nature. . . . The urges show also in the artistic abilities, and the ability to design of every character, anew, as it were, from others, for much of the Temple decorations in that day were of the mind of this entity. . . .")

177

To continue the chronicle of this family, let's look now at a reading given on July 1, 1930 for Barbara Withers, who was to marry Charles Morrison six years later. They had known each other for several years, and were dating at the time the reading was given. (On the day they met, Barbara came home from school and exclaimed to her mother, "He's the most wonderful boy! I love him. I know that sounds silly—but I feel as though I've known him for a long, long time.")

Concerning Barbara, Cayce said, "In the appearance before this we find during that period when there were troublesome times in the land known as France. The entity then the one to whom the young King [the Dauphin] was given in charge, and was the keeper of same—even until the time of the passing from the body. The entity lost and gained through that influence. During the first portion of this period the entity lost, for oft were the stripes laid on the body [of the Dauphin] by the entity. Then in the latter period were there the sorrows as were known from the conditions as surrounded that brought for the entity much of an understanding of the better relationships between those of high estate and those that were of the keeper, or the servant, in such periods."

So we find that in her French incarnation, Barbara had been in charge of the young man who would have been King Louis XVII, had the Revolution not intervened. Generally, the assumption has been that her position was that of nursemaid. However, in this reading Cayce departed from his usual practice and did not furnish her name for that incarnation. Since the sex of the entity was rarely designated in the readings, an interesting point is raised.

There has always been some question concerning the fate of the young Dauphin following the execution of his parents. Rumors have persisted, but have never been substantiated, that he escaped the country. However, the records of the French government indicate that he was placed in the care of a cobbler named Simon, suffered neglect, and died at the age of ten. Considering the complete confusion existing in France in the years of the Revolution, it is possible that the records are incorrect. It is equally possible, of course, that Cayce erred in stating that the Dauphin died at the age of fifteen.

Noting Cayce's harsh statements in Barbara's reading concerning the person caring for the Dauphin, we wonder if possibly she was the person the French records show as "Simon." Cayce's remarks to the effect that the Dauphin was often whipped, and suffered much, would make this seem plausible. His statement that she had been with the Dauphin until the time of his death does raise this perplexing question: was Barbara a man in that incarnation—a man named Simon? Or was she, as has been assumed, a nursemaid—possibly one who was in the French court, later took the boy to Simon, and stayed on, thus sharing in the care (and neglect) of the child until his death? Spanking a child occasionally—or even often—would not seem to be sufficient basis for Cayce's claiming that the entity (now Barbara) had suffered soul retrogression which was somewhat cancelled out by an understanding, later in her life, "of the better relationships between those of high estate and those that were . . . the servant in such periods."

Barbara's sister received a life reading in December, 1930. Said Cayce, "In the one before this we find during that period when there were rebellions or oppressions in the land known as the French. The entity was among those peoples who were in touch with those in authority as rulers, for the entity [was] one of the offspring [of those] to whom these peoples went upon their attempt to escape from the land. . . ."

Taken by itself, this statement doesn't particularly advance our knowledge of French history. It undoubtedly refers to the known fact that, on the night of June 20, 1791, the King and Queen and their family, disguised as ordinary travelers, went by coach toward Malmédy on the eastern border of France. They were detected at Varennes, and were forced to return to Paris.

This episode in history was elaborated on in a Cayce reading given in October, 1939, for Charles and Barbara Morrison's daughter. "Before that we find the entity was in the French land; being a child, or a young lady thirteen to fourteen years of age in the experience, when the en-

179

tity's present father and its present mother (an attendant to the present father) were, with the King and the Queen, turned back."

(This statement, of course, shoots a few holes in our speculations about the possibility that Barbara, in her French incarnation, had been a cobbler named Simon to whom the Dauphin was given in charge. It does not rule out the possibility that she later went with the Dauphin to Simon—or, indeed, that there *was* no Simon, after all; that the French records are wrong. We could have eliminated all mention of such speculations on our part, but instead we have included them to show the kind of thing many people went through upon receiving their readings and, trying to match up what Cayce had to say with what has been recorded in history, found mystifying discrepancies.)

To continue the reading for Barbara's daughter, we find that Cayce said, "The entity was then in the household of the tavern where that turning back took place—in the name then Arabela.

"In the experience the entity suffered through its feelings for those who were to the entity so royal, so above others; and, because of their gentleness, their kindness, their feelings, the entity has sought expression in such environs in the present. . . ." (There was an unusually strong tie between this child and her grandmother, the "former" Marie Antoinette. Her grandfather died before the child was born.)

The Morrisons also had a son. His life reading, interestingly enough, shows no French incarnation—although he had been associated with some members of his family in an early appearance in Egypt.

When these readings are put together, it is easy to see that Cayce has furnished a good portion of French history. Presented over a span of some *fourteen years,* he has given facts concerning each individual which, combined with facts given to other members of the family, form a complete story. There are no deviations from accepted facts concerning the French royal family, with the exception noted above concerning the fate of the Dauphin. (Later readings were given for the purpose of expanding this information, and although much was added, nothing was altered.)

180

All these statements were made spontaneously during the course of the readings. None came as a result of direct questioning or prompting of any kind.

The Essenes and the Dead Sea Scrolls

There are a number of Cayce readings on file in which an individual was said to have been connected, in a former incarnation, with an Essene community. These readings gave much information concerning such communities which at that time could not be confirmed.

This was because, at the time of the readings, hardly anything was known of the Essenes. What little was known came principally from the writings of three men, all of whom lived during the first century after the birth of Christ: the Jewish historian, Josephus; the philosopher, Philo; and the Roman historian, Pliny the Elder.

What made things even more confusing was that often what Cayce said about the entity's experience during that time did not match up completely with what was known about the Essenes, or, for that matter, what we know about them today.

Present knowledge—admittedly still scanty—has it that the Essenes were a Jewish religious group which flourished in the two centuries before and after the period of Christ's appearance on the earth. They were a communal society, extremely pious, who emphasized the virtue of physical and spiritual purity. They refused to take oaths or engage in animal sacrifices as did the Sadducees and the Pharisees. Their major endeavors centered around agriculture and handicrafts, for they felt these two occupations were the least sinful. They abhorred commerce, believing that it led to the covetousness and to the making of the weapons of war. Until recent years, when skeletons of women were found in the graveyards of some Essene communities, it was believed that they were inhabited only by men. (This, incidentally, confirmed statements made years earlier by Cayce.)

The Essenes were thought by some to be celibate, but their numbers did not die out because of the practice of taking in young boys and bringing them up as novices, as well as accepting adult males who rejected life outside the communities. Enrichment of the soul was the main em-

181

phasis of their religion. It has been widely speculated—although not yet proved—that John the Baptist was an Essene.

The Essenes were highly respected, and became famous for their mysticism and esoteric knowledge—the nature of which is little known, since the Essene communities were essentially secret societies.

There has been much controversy, through the years, concerning whether or not Jesus Christ was associated with the Essenes. Although there is no consequential evidence to support either side of the debate, the consensus seems to be that Jesus was not connected with them, but that some of his disciples may have come out of such communities—particularly those who were formerly disciples of John the Baptist.

The Cayce readings, however, indicate otherwise. Bearing in mind that there can be no proof, as yet, of the accuracy of what he had to say on the subject, here is a brief rundown of the life of Jesus as it is shown in the Cayce files.

First we should mention that Cayce, in his many discussions of the Essenes through the readings, said that in Palestine their principal center was at Mount Carmel, near the shores of the Mediterranean Sea. (Practically no archaeological surveys have been done in this area, as yet; it is interesting to speculate on what might be uncovered in future years.)

Here is what Cayce had to say in one reading. "In the days when more and more leaders of the people had been trained in the temple at Mount Carmel, the original place where the school of the prophets was established during Elijah's time, there were those leaders called Essenes —students of what ye would call astronomy, astrology, phrenology, numbers and numerology, and that study of the return of individuals—or reincarnation.

"There were reasons why these proclaimed that certain periods formed a cycle—reasons which grew out of the studies of Aristotle, Enos, Mathias, Judy and others who supervised the school, as ye would term it in the present.

"These individuals had been persecuted by leaders of the people, and this caused the saying of which ye have an interpretation, as given by the Sadducees, 'There is no resurrection' or 'There is no reincarnation'—which is what the word meant in those days. . . .

"Hence there was continued preparation and dedication of those who might be channels through whom the chosen vessel could enter—through choice—into materiality. Those in charge at that time were Mathias, Enos and Judy. Thus in Carmel where there were the priests of this faith . . . twelve maidens were chosen who were dedicated to this purpose, this office, this service. Among them was Mary, the beloved, the chosen one; and she, as had been foretold, was chosen as the channel. Thus she was separated and kept in closer associations with and in the care of this office.

"That was the beginning, that was the foundation of what ye term the Church."

According to the readings, then, it was the Essenes who chose Mary to be the Virgin Mother. She had been chosen at the age of four, and had been placed in the custody of the temple priests at Carmel. There she had begun a long and arduous training period which included mental and physical exercises, special foods and diet, learning the wisdom and necessity of chastity, purity, love, patience and endurance. She was twelve before she was told the purpose of her training.

The readings indicate that Joseph, also selected by the Essenes, objected at first to the union with Mary. He was, after all, thirty-six years old, whereas Mary was only sixteen. He was concerned about what people would say, not only because of the difference in their ages, but because of the very nature of a virgin birth. However, through a dream and a vision he became convinced that it was Divine Will, and he consented.

The marriage ceremony, said Cayce, was performed at Carmel in the temple of the Essenes, after which Joseph returned to his home in Nazareth and Mary retired to the hill country of Judea to await the birth of Jesus.

Near the end of her pregnancy, Mary joined Joseph at Nazareth and they began the journey to Bethany—some seventy miles away—to register for taxation as required by law.

It was about this time that the wise men, who were initiates in the Mysteries, perceived the signs of the coming of Jesus, and came from Egypt, India and the Gobi, to serve as emissaries of the religious leaders in those countries. They bore their gifts of gold, frankincense and myrrh, representing, according to Cayce, the healing force —or body, mind and soul.

Then, at midnight on January 6 of the present Gregorian calendar, Jesus was born in the stable of a hillside inn in Bethlehem. The inkeeper's daughter acted as midwife.

One reading elaborated on this journey to Bethany. "Each individual was required by Roman law to be present in the city of his birth for this polling. Both Joseph and Mary were members of the sect called Essenes; and thus they were to be polled and questioned not only by those in political, but also in religious authority in the City. . . .

"For remember, many of those present [at the inn] were also of that questioned group, the Essenes. They had heard of the girl, that lovely wife of Joseph, who had been chosen by the angel on the stair; they had heard of what had taken place in the hills where Elizabeth had gone, when she [Elizabeth] had been visited by this girl, her cousin . . ."

According to the readings, Mary had spent the required period of purification following the birth of Jesus. Then the Infant had been taken to the temple to be blessed by Anna, Mary's mother, and by the high priest. The family then returned to Nazareth. Herod's edict, ordering the death of the Jews, had forced them to flee to Egypt; they remained there for five years. A handmaid called Josie, and at other times called Sophie, stayed with Mary for many years, helping with the care of the young Jesus, as well as with the other children who came later. She also cared for Joseph in his last days. Josie was an Essene; thus the readings indicate a continuing influence of the Essenes upon the life of Jesus.

After the five-year stay in Egypt, the family went to Judea, then to Capernaum, and then settled once again in Nazareth. At the age of ten, Jesus was presented in the temple. There was much counseling and discussion among the rabbis, leading to Jesus' going to Egypt to begin His schooling in the secret doctrines of the law. The readings do not specify whether or not these rabbis were Essenes; however, they do indicate that Jesus had some teaching by the Essenes.

"The return was made to Capernaum, not Nazareth, and not just because of political reasons following the death of Herod. But a division of the kingdom had been made after the death of Herod. And the return [to Capernaum] was so that there might be the ministry or teaching that was to be a part of the Brotherhood, supervised in that period by Judy, as one of the leaders of the Essenes in that particular period."

According to the readings, Jesus spent only a short time in Egypt in connection with His training. He was then sent to India, and then "into what is now Persia."

Jesus spent one year in Egypt, India and Persia. He was called home upon the death of Joseph, and then returned to Egypt for more schooling. The readings indicate that during part of this time He was with John the Messenger. Between the ages of thirteen and sixteen, He was in India and studied under Kshijiar. In Persia He studied under Junner; in Egypt, under Zar.

Then, "after the return to Jerusalem there were the periods of education in Syria, India and the completion of the studies in Egypt; and the passing of the tests there by those who were of the Essene group, as they entered into the service; as did the Master, and John before him."

Once His schooling was completed, Jesus went to Capernaum, Cana and the land of Judea. Here the readings coincide with what has been written in the Gospels concerning Jesus' ministry. He taught the lessons of Isaiah, Jeremiah and the lesser prophets, in the synagogues.

Jesus, as portrayed in the readings, was not of the sad countenance and frail body generally depicted by others. Indeed, said Cayce, He smiled often, and sometimes spoke lightly. He excelled in playing the harp.

He attended the wedding of his sister Ruth, who married a Roman tax supervisor.

There are a great many readings given for individuals which support the story of Jesus and fill in many gaps in present knowledge of the Essenes.

A summary of this information might contain the following: there were many Essene communities, widely scattered throughout the Middle East area, from Egypt to India. In Palestine, their center was not on the Dead Sea, but at Mount Carmel, some seventy miles to the north.

Although Jesus, according to the readings, was raised and educated by Essenes, He seems to have differed with them in some aspects of their beliefs. Indeed, some of His admonishments seem to have been directed toward them.

The readings indicate that the Essene community on the Dead Sea was evidently dispersed around 70 A.D., when large numbers of Roman soldiers drove them from their site.

With the discovery of the Dead Sea Scrolls of Khirbet Qumran in 1947, and the extensive excavations of the various caves in the area since that time, we now seem to be on the way to finding out whether Cayce's readings were completely accurate, partly accurate, or absolutely wrong. So far, there seems to have been no discovery that disproves what he had to say. Some discoveries have confirmed material given in the readings.

Restoring the Scrolls—tens of thousands of bits of papyrus, copper and leather, in a dreadful state of decay—is a monumental task, and it has been estimated that it may take at least fifty years to decipher and translate those already recovered. Even as this is accomplished, there will surely be growing debates concerning their content and their meaning to Christianity.

One piece of Essene literature recently deciphered indicates that the communion meal of that day, almost identical to that used today, was a liturgical anticipation of the Messianic banquet. It details the offering of the bread, and then the wine, to the congregation of the community. It ends with the statement, "And they shall follow this prescription whenever [the meal is ar]ranged, when as many as ten meet together."

The Last Supper Described by Edgar Cayce

The foregoing was not presented as a means of trying to establish proof of the accuracy of Cayce's readings concerning Jesus. Such an attempt would be, at the least, extremely premature. But because of information coming to light as a result of the discovery of the Dead Sea Scrolls, we thought you would find Cayce's words interesting. The same might be said for the following reading.

It was given at the end of a physical reading for a woman on June 14, 1932. Cayce, after being given the suggestion to awaken three times, refused to do so. Instead, he began to recite this story of the Last Supper:

"Here, with the Master. See what they have for supper . . . boiled fish, rice with leeks, wine, and loaf. One of the pitchers in which it is served is broken. The handle is broken as is the lip to same.

"The whole robe of the Master is not white, but pearl gray—all combined into one—the gift of Nicodemus to the Lord.

"The better looking of the twelve, of course, was Judas. The younger was John: oval face, dark hair, smooth face, the only one with the short hair. Peter, the rough and ready, always that of very short beard, rough, and not altogether clean. Andrew's is just the opposite: very sparse, but inclined to be long more on the side and under the chin—long on the upper lip. His robe was always near gray or black, while his clouts or breeches were striped; while those of Philip and Bartholomew were red and brown.

"The Master's hair is 'most red, inclined to be curly in portions, yet not feminine or weak. Strong, with heavy piercing eyes that are blue or steel-gray.

"His weight would be at least a hundred and seventy pounds. Long, tapering fingers, nails well kept. Long nail, though, on the left little finger.

"Merry—even in the hour of trial. Joke—even in the moment of betrayal.

"The sack is empty. Judas departs.

"The last is given of the wine and loaf, with which He gives the emblems that should be so dear to every follower of Him. Lays aside His robe, which is all of one piece. Girds the towel about His waist, which is dressed with linen that is blue and white. Rolls back the folds, kneels first before John, James, then to Peter—who refuses.

"Then the dissertation as to 'He that would be the greatest would be servant of all."

"The basin taken is without handle, and is made of

wood. The water is from the gherkins, that are in the wide-mouth shibboleths that stand in the house of John's father, Zebedee.

"And now comes, 'It is finished.'

"They sing the ninety-first Psalm: 'He that dwelleth in the secret place of the Most High shall abide under the shadow of the Almighty. I will say of the Lord, He is my refuge and my fortress; my God, in Him will I trust.'

"He is the musician as well, for He uses the harp.

"They leave for the garden."

Here again, as in the case of the Essenes, and Jesus' connection with them, we find that Cayce has provided a most interesting situation. He has interwoven accepted versions of Biblical history and material supplied from his own source of information, presumably the akashic records.

His version of the last Supper is unique, so far as we can determine. It agrees in some respects with the accounts given in the four Gospels—which, themselves, do not completely agree—and seems to be an attempt to fill out the story for us, to expand our knowledge of this important and moving event.

It would be difficult, if not impossible, to believe that such a narration amounted to nothing more than a fanciful journey through the unconscious mind of Edgar Cayce.

Who Built Stonehenge—And When?

The famous ruined monument—now no more than a complex arrangement of ditches, pits and stone columns on England's Salisbury plain—continues to be a mystery.

My 200-year-old Encyclopaedia Britannica indicates that around 1768 Stonehenge consisted of "the remains of four ranks of rough stones, ranged one within another, some of them, especially in the outermost and third rank, twenty feet high, and seven broad; sustaining others laid across their heads and fastened by mortises, so that the whole must have anciently hung together . . ."

In those days, people were pretty well convinced that it was a British temple. However, said the encyclopaedia, the English architect Inigo Jones had "given a fine scheme of the work, and strives hard to persuade the world that it was Roman."

In 1797, amateur archaeological expeditions caused some of the enormous stones to topple to the ground.

Then, in 1950, the theory that the monument had been built by Druids was finally laid to rest. Interest, which had flagged over the centuries, was revived.

In 1952, Professor W. F. Libby of the University of Chicago estimated that Stonehenge had been constructed about 3,800 years before, or around 1850 B.C.

In 1958, Richard J. C. Atkinson reported his view that the monuments were not of British design or construction, but the work of "an itinerant architect from one of the two great Mediterranean civilizations—the Minoan in Crete or the Mycenean in Greece." Mr. Atkinson, together with Professor Stuart Piggott, had been put in charge of a British-financed project to raise the six 45-ton stones which had fallen in 1797.

In 1959, the British Museum announced that radiocarbon dating of bits of deer antler found at Stonehenge proved that the monuments had been built around 3,670 years before. In other words, they supported the estimate of Professor Libby.

In 1964, Dr. Gerald Hawkins of the Smithsonian Astrophysical Observatory reported on experiments he had made which indicated that Stonehenge may have been a huge astronomical calendar. He calculated the directions of the lines joining the various stones and holes of the compound, gathered data relative to the movements and positions of the heavenly bodies at the time Stonehenge was built (1500 B.C., according to his estimate) and fed this data into a computer. The results showed twenty-four close correlations with solar and lunar directions. Dr. Hawkins, said the report, is convinced that Stonehenge was built as a device for predicting seasons and for signalling the approach of eclipses. This, he said, indicated a remarkably advanced solar-lunar lore, in some ways superior to that of the Egyptians and Mesopotamians of the period.

The mystery would seem to be still quite a mystery.

So let's turn to what Edgar Cayce had to say about Stonehenge in several readings given in which the subject came up.

In one, he was asked outright to tell who built

Stonehenge, and for what purpose.

He answered, "In the Holy Land when there were those dredgings up in the period when the land was being sacked by the Chaldeans and Persians . . . among those groups who escaped in ships and settled in portions of the English land near what is now Salisbury, and there builded those altars that were to represent the dedication of individuals to the service of a living God."

In other words, Stonehenge was built around 1800 B.C. by Jews escaping the Chaldeans and Persians. This date would seem to agree with the estimates of Professor Libby and the British Museum.

Another time, Cayce said, "Before that the entity was in England . . . and there should be many of those lands, especially in the areas where altars were once set up by the peoples from the Holy Land, that should be of interest as well as bring to the mind of the consciousness of the entity the happenings of that period. . . ."

And in another reading, "in the land of the present nativity [England] during those periods when there was the expanding of the activities of the groups that had settled there from the Holy Land . . . A home builder, in the name Ersa Kent. . . ."

Still another reading stated, "Before this the entity was in England when the people from the Holy Land were coming in. The entity was with a group which had been part of the temple watch in Jerusalem, which had established the outer courts of the temple for individual service and activity. The entity helped set up altars which long since have been torn away, though evidence yet remains of stones set up in the form of a court, with an inner court for those who sought to learn of the Lord." Thus, in this reading, Edgar Cayce described not only the earlier temple, but the ruins as they appear today!

In another reading he said, ". . . before that we find the entity was in the English land in the early settlings of the children of Israel who were foregathered with the daughters of Hezekiah in what is now Somerland, Somerhill, or Somerset. There the entity saw group organization for the preservation of tenets and truths of the Living God. . . ."

And finally, this: "Before that the entity was in the

English land during those periods when there was the breaking up of the tribes of Israel. The entity was a granddaughter of Hezekiah the King, and among those who set sail to escape when the activities brought the rest of the people into servitude in the Persian land. Then the entity was among those who landed and set up the seat of customs as indicated in the altars built near what is now Salisbury, England."

These readings were for different individuals, given over a considerable span of years. And yet the information in each of them seems to parallel all the others. Although this, in itself, cannot prove the accuracy of the readings, it certainly makes a thought-provoking statement.

CHAPTER THIRTEEN

PRECOGNITION AND PROPHECY

Edgar Cayce certainly did not consider himself a prophet. And yet he uttered, over a period of some forty-three years, an almost incredible number of prophetic statements—a great many of which have already come true.

In scope, these statements seem limitless. They range all the way from a simple one, made at the end of a physical reading for a woman suffering from a severe cold, "Then—be well by Wednesday!" to a complex and frightening one indicating that great earth changes would begin to take place during the period 1958 to 1998. The woman with the cold *was* completely well by Wednesday. And a lot of the earth changes prophesied by Edgar Cayce *have begun.*

There are enough Cayce prophecies on file to fill a book. Fortunately, they do fill one: a book in this series, entitled, *Edgar Cayce on Prophecy.* Since its author, Mary Ellen Carter, has done a fine job of pulling this material together and putting it into focus, we will not attempt to cover the subject in any depth within this chapter. Instead, we will try to indicate the scope of the material by citing a few examples from the Cayce readings.

Prophecy: Concerning the Individual

Edgar Cayce, in 1934, was asked if it is possible, by psychic means, to absolutely prophesy specific events in the future of an individual.

He answered, "Such things should rather be builded from within. And if the soul merits such [success], through that it metes to its fellow man, it will bring such into the experience of the body. But to say that it *will* happen—it can't be done! For the Father, Himself, has given each soul that portion of Himself. What the soul *does* about his knowledge, about his abilities or opportunities, depends upon the *will* of the soul.

"Hence, as to whether this is to come to pass or may not come to pass—it may, my brother, to *any* soul. What wilt thou do about the opportunities that have been and are being presented to thee?"

So we see that Cayce's words concerning the future of an individual were never to be considered fortune telling. Rather, and this is particularly evident in the life readings, Cayce told of personal characteristics and talents as he "read" them from the person's unconscious mind. It was then up to the individual to do something about his talents, to make the most of the opportunities that came his way. If the reading indicated a need for caution in certain areas, then it was up to the individual to exercise such caution. Nevertheless, a great many statements Cayce made in the life readings seemed prophetic—and were proven by the passage of time. This is because the individual followed his reading, or his natural bent, or both.

In the physical readings, a statement such as, "Then—be well by Wednesday!" meant simply, "This is the best treatment for this particular body. Follow it faithfully, with the correct mental attitude, and you will be well." If the patient obeyed instructions, the "prophecy" generally came true.

We have seen many examples of such statements contained in readings covered in earlier chapters; indeed, some degree of prophecy is to be found in the majority of life and physical readings. But we did not specifically point to certain portions of the readings and exclaim, "Prophecy!" We will do so now, with a couple of interesting readings from the Cayce files.

John Marshall's reading was given when he was only eight months old, and yet we find that Cayce was most explicit—and prophetic—in suggesting his career potentials. "We find those influences will be in the direction of mathematical calculations," he said. "Especially as pertaining to electrical energy." The parents were directed to give the boy every opportunity to develop interest in mathematics and electricity. "Then we would find the wonderful mental development of the entity in the present earth's plane. . . ."

"In the urge as will be found in the present entity: that of the ability to correlate data in a manner that will be at fingertips, as it were, in memory and mathematical form . . . .

"Then, that to which the entity may attain in the present earth's plane, and how: with the correct guiding through the moulding age, the entity will take on those urges of the electrical forces and application of same in a mathematical manner beyond that as has been undertaken heretofore . . ."

At the age of fourteen, John Marshall announced to his mother that he intended to become an airplane designer. He took a part-time job in an electric shop.

When he was nineteen, John's mother wrote to A.R.E. to say that he was working with the Air Transport Command as an aviation mechanic. He was also attending night school.

When John was twenty-nine, his mother reported that he had gone into partnership in an electrical construction business. "He likes it very much, and is doing well," she said.

Three years later, she indicated that John's abilities were still being cultivated, even at the age of thirty-two. "He goes to college two nights a week, still taking physics. He has to study other evenings and also puts in some overtime. He is now a Production Engineer. I believe he will be married soon. . . ."

It is evident from the correspondence that John Marshall's road was not paved with gold, and that he pretty much had to make his own opportunities. He had to work hard to reach the potential indicated in the Cayce reading, but he accomplished it with singleminded determination. He is married now, with children, and has become highly successful in his field as well as in his family and social life.

In contrast, consider the case of Peter Matson, who was given a life reading in 1944. He was twelve years old. Cayce had many warnings concerning his future. "In giving the interpretations of the records here of this entity, it would be very easy to interpret same either in a very optimistic or a very pessimistic vein. For there are great possibilities and great obstacles. But know, in either case, the real lesson is within self. For here is the opportunity for an entity (while comparisons are odious, these would be good comparisons) to be either a Beethoven or a Whittier or a Jesse James or some such entity! For the entity is inclined to think more highly of himself than he ought to think, as would be indicated. That's what these three individuals did, in themselves. As to the application made of it, depends upon the individual self."

Cayce indicated that Peter had a strong latent ability to become a musician, a poet or a writer, "which few would ever excel. Or there may be the desire to have its own way to such an extent that the entity will be in the position to disregard others altogether in every form, just so self has its own way."

Depending upon how well the boy might be brought under control, without breaking his spirit, Cayce said, "we will not only give to the world a real individual with genius, but make for individual soul development. Otherwise, we will give to the world one of genius in making trouble for somebody."

Peter's parents tried very hard to follow the reading. They sent him to a strict boarding school, and sought professional help for their son in an attempt to understand and guide his difficult personality.

At the age of sixteen, however, Peter became emotionally unbalanced. Three years later, he shot his father and his grandmother. He was confined to a mental hospital for several years.

In 1956, when Peter was twenty-four, his mother reported to A.R.E. that, although Peter was still in an institution, she was optimistic about his future. "With only one setback, he has steadily improved and we have great hopes that he will ultimately recover. . . ."

We certainly would not want to imply that anyone could have done anything to prevent the tragedy in Peter's life. His parents spared no effort or expense in getting the best professional help available for this young man both before and after his emotional problems erupted in violence.

Rather, we offer the case to illustrate how well Cayce

foretold, through explaining the natural inclinations of twelve-year-old Peter Matson, the difficulties that lay ahead.

Prophecy: Concerning the Human Body

Philip Andrews was suffering from a serious form of arthritis which affected his back and legs. In one of a series of readings given for this condition, Cayce was asked if the prescribed treatments would check the atrophying of the muscles in Philip's right leg and thigh.

"They will check the atrophying of the muscles in the limbs," he stated.

"Can the leg be brought back to normal?"

"Try it!" Cayce said. "It's worth trying! It will, if there are the applications in the manners indicated."

This statement was made on September 12, 1937. Exactly one month later, Philip wrote to Edgar Cayce, "First of all, there was immediate relief as a result of the treatment outlined in my last reading. The leg, which was rapidly atrophying, has put on flesh, and Dr. D. is amazed at it. . . ."

This is not an unusual case at all. The A.R.E. files are full of such prophetic statements which came true *because of the application made by the individual*—the one ingredient stressed in the Cayce readings as being essential to success.

In the physical readings, both those for individuals and those covering a specific malady for which a special reading was given (such as the common cold) we find much prophecy—although often it is so subtle that it might easily be missed, had it not been repeated so often.

For example, Edgar Cayce prescribed the use of gold, in various forms, for use in many different illnesses.

The sands at Virginia Beach, he said, contained much chloride of gold, and arthritis patients, particularly, were directed to lie on the beach with affected portions of the body covered by the sand in order to let the sun "bake" it in. (My grandfather was one of these, and it helped him immeasurably.)

Chloride of gold, said Cayce in a reading given many years ago, would be particularly useful in "any condition wherein there is any form of the condition bordering on rheumatics, or of the necessity of rejuvenating any organ of the system showing the delinquency in action, see?"

In the same reading, he stated, "Many of the conditions as are existent in alcoholic stimulants, as have been applied to the system, that has destroyed the tissue in central portion of the body, destroyed tissue in the recreative forces in the generative system, destroyed tissue in other portions of the system, even unto the brain itself, give these (the various ails of the body); gold or silver, or both, would add and rebuild—rejuvenate, as it were, in the system. Give these, for they are good."

Among many conditions for which chloride of gold was specified by Cayce in his readings were the physical problems associated with alcoholism, arthritis, assimilations, asthenia, blindness, bursitis, cancer, circulatory disturbances, diverticulitis, eliminations, glands, insanity, menopause, multiple sclerosis, and so on. In some cases it was to be administered orally. In others, it was to be given through use of a so-called "wet cell appliance," a vibratory device developed out of the Cayce readings which, in effect, electrically transmitted certain substances into the body—or, as suggested in at least one reading, enabled inactive elements in the body, such as gold, to become stimulated into action.

The main factor in the specification of gold in the readings seems to be that gold has a rejuvenating power for the body. Its use, as shown in many readings, goes back over a period of many years.

Four years ago, we began to get reports of the use of gold by "orthodox" medicine. A report in *Science News Letter* of October 3, 1964, carried the information that electrically charged gold leaves, *used for the first time on humans and animals* [author's italics] in a Washington, D. C., hospital, had been found to prevent troublesome adhesions and to patch blood vessels!

According to this report, fractures had been successfully treated in that way. "And," said the article, "in some cases it can replace silk sutures as well as form a protective layer over surgical suture lines." (Silk sutures can cause an adverse tissue reaction, whereas gold leaf has been proved not to do so.)

This success led to a review of medical literature, which disclosed the fact that gold salts had been used in the treatment of disease, especially arthritis; gold leaves—not electrically charged, however—had been applied to the pustules of smallpox to prevent scarring; gold foil had been used for the healing and closing of perforations of the eardrum; and gold plate had been used to cover a defect in the cranium.

In the Washington, D. C., *Sunday Star,* dateline September 5, 1965, there was this statement: "Doctors here are fashioning the fanciest bandages ever—out of gold leaf.

" 'Nobody knows why,' one said. 'But damn it, it works!'

"It seems to relieve pain and stop the oozing from severe burns and skin ulcers and sores. Best of all, it apparently speeds the wounds' healing.

"Deep wounds as big around as a hand seem to start healing in a couple of days in some cases, the doctors say.

"Patients who might ordinarily be expected to heal only after weeks or months in a hospital are sometimes able to continue work while letting the gold do its work."

The newspaper account continued with a description of a surgical technique developed by Doctors John P. Gallagher and Charles F. Geschickter which had been perfected through use on experimental animals. Dr. Gallagher had later used the technique on a nine-year-old boy with severe head injuries, and thereby saved his life.

The technique had been reported in the *Journal* of the American Medical Association and, said the news report, was now being used by a number of physicians and surgeons.

The *Sunday Star* report continued with news of work being done at the Hebrew Home for the Aged in Washington, D. C. in which thin sheets of gold had been applied to big, open wounds and sores with spectacular results. It mentioned the experiences of Dr. Naomi M. Kanof, a dermatologist, who had been getting good results with the application of gold leaf to "long-standing, deep and open skin ulcers resulting from injuries, diabetic and varicose conditions, and from the deterioration known by the mild name of 'bedsores.' "

Also, said the report, Dr. Linwood L. Rayford, Jr., of Washington, D. C., had "transferred the gold leaf technique into the treatment of large, painful second degree burns. In the severest case, the burns covered 25 percent of the patient's body.

"The gold, Rayford said, cuts the severe pain and dries the wound—from which burn patients ordinarily may lose important body fluids."

The news report quoted Dr. Rayford as saying, "I have the impression that it also quickens the healing."

It is difficult to look at Cayce readings dealing with the use of gold, and then at subsequent reports of the advances of "modern" medicine, and affix a tag which reads "prophecy." Maybe this is because we generally think of prophecy as being manifested in an individual who says, "I predict . . ." or "I see in the future . . ." This is not what Edgar Cayce did at all. He merely used techniques and substances that "orthodox" medicine did not come to use until a number of years after Cayce specified them in his readings. Thus his *work,* and not simply his *words,* could be said to have been prophetic.

There is a wealth of such evidence in the files, and there is hardly an area, within the broad concept of bodily health, that is not touched on in some way.

The dietary advice, alone, as given in the Cayce readings, was at least a generation ahead of its time. We referred to this in an earlier chapter in discussing the orange juice specified in massive doses for a young boy with leukemia; in Cayce's words concerning the food value to be found in coffee; and in other such instances.

Concerning coffee, by the way, Cayce said that not only was it a food when taken *without* cream or milk, but that *with* cream or milk it might well harm the digestion. This kind of statement was repeated, again and again, is many readings for individuals. It seemed curiously eccentric advice.

However, in the Sunday Magazine Section of the *Philadelphia Inquirer* dated March 9, 1958, we find this item: "If you suffer dyspeptic distress after drinking coffee, it may be caused by the cream. Doctors at the University of Turku, Finland, have concluded that upset stomach results more from coffee with cream than from black coffee alone."

Cayce often urged against the indiscriminate use of vitamin supplements, maintaining that vitamins were properly to be obtained from an adequate, nutritious diet. Whenever he specified vitamin pills or tonics, he indicated that they were to be taken for a stated period, then left off in order to prevent the body's becoming dependent upon them. Otherwise, he said, the system would cease to assimilate and manufacture vitamins from even the most adequate diet. "It is much better for these vitamins to be produced in the body," he explained, "from the normal development, than supplied mechanically, for nature is much better, still, than science!"

Many years later, in February, 1961, the American Medical Association issued a warning: don't munch too many vitamin pills! The *Journal* of the A.M.A., reporting a widespread belief that people must consume multivitamin pills to keep healthy, stated, "On the contrary, only in a deficiency state or in an anticipated deficiency state are vitamin supplements necessary." An overdose of vitamins, added the *Journal,* can cause loss of appetite, irritability, skin eruptions, liver enlargement, and gastrointestinal symptoms.

Cayce once stated, concerning the acid-alkaline balance in the human body, "Overalkalinity is much more harmful than a little tendency for acidity."

In a report in the *National Health Federation Bulletin* of December, 1962, Dr. George A. Wilson stated that, as a result of tests he had made on hundreds of patients of the renowned Spears Chiropractic Hospital in Denver, Colorado, over a fourteen-year period, and backed up by his forty-five years of experience, he was convinced that most sick people are too alkaline, rather than too acid, as has generally been thought. This was found to be especially true of people with chronic illnesses, he said.

And consider: almost twenty-five years ago, Edgar Cayce said this about human blood: "There is no condition existent in a body, the reflection of which may not be traced in the blood supply. Not only does the blood stream carry the rebuilding forces to the body; it takes the used forces and eliminates them through their proper channels in the various portions of the system. We find red blood, white blood and lymph, all carried in the veins. These are only separated by the very small portions that act as builders, strainers, destroyers, or resuscitating portions of the system. For there is always seen in the blood stream the reflection or the evidence of that condition being enacted in the physical body. *The day may yet arrive when one may take a drop of blood and diagnose the condition of any physical body*." [Author's italics.]

On March 20, 1958, a story was carried in the Norfolk (Virginia) *Virginian-Pilot* concerning research being conducted by Dr. Winston Price at Johns Hopkins Hospital on medical diagnosis, involving analysis of particles in the blood stream. Said the report, "His discovery could mean that a medical laboratory can tell what ails you—cancer, tuberculosis, ulcers, or even mental disorders—*simply by examination of a drop of your blood*." [Author's italics.]

On February 16, 1960, the Washington (D.C.) *Daily News* ran a short feature describing a method of analyzing a single drop of blood or a tiny bit of tissue to identify the enzymes present.

By means of a so-called "zymograph," said the paper, its developers—Doctors R. L. Hunter and C. L. Markest, working at the University of Michigan with financial support of the American Cancer Society, hoped that it would be "possible, by observing and analyzing the enzymes in the blood, to trace the changes which take place in the process of growth from the embryonic state to old age."

By studying the chemical changes that accompany various diseases, then, the doctors felt it might in time be possible to diagnose some diseases, possibly even cancer, before clinical symptoms have appeared.

Business Week, on November 21, 1964, covered this same subject. The magazine reported that Dr. John B. Henry, Professor of Pathology at the Medical Center of New York, Syracuse, speaking before a meeting of the American College of Clinical Pathologists in New York, had discussed the role of enzymes in diagnosing disease.

The article stated that it had been known for some time that the quantity of enzymes in the blood and other body fluids could be used to measure cell death or damage. For example, cancer sometimes produces high enzyme levels, whereas lower enzyme levels might indicate some other type of disease.

Dr. Henry's ultimate hope, said this story, was that some day a series of laboratory tests—a single enzyme "profile"—might be developed as a kind of chart for use in conjunction with blood tests to determine, within a matter of hours, the presence of any of a number of possible diseases.

About a year and a half earlier, *Business Week* (March 9, 1963) had also reported a new diagnostic test to detect Wilson's disease, a rare malady that strikes people of all ages and is often diagnosed as mental or emotional illness.

The test was developed by the Albert Einstein College of Medicine in New York. Doctors there were reported as saying that, if detected early enough, Wilson's disease should be treatable with drugs, diet and psychotherapy.

The test, said the report, now made it possible to detect the presence of the disease before the appearance of any clinical signs. *All that is needed for the test is one drop of blood from the patient.*

These, of course, are only a few examples out of the Cayce files to illustrate the kind of prophetic material that may be found there. Considering this, we wonder if it isn't just a matter of time before the "orthodox" medical world catches up with the "Cayce" medical world and supplies the scientific facts behind a great many more of his statements.

For starters, in the dietary department, how about these?

Cayce frequently insisted that certain foods should not be combined at the same meal (e.g. citrus fruits or juices with wheat cereals.) Why?

Cayce specified that fruits and vegetables are more easily assimilated into the body when combined with gelatin. Why?

Cayce made the flat-out statement, many years ago, that within the blueberry there is "a property which someone, someday, will use in its proper place!" What is this property?

Prophecy: Is It Rooted in History?

Suppose, for the moment, that you are living in the year

1934. You are sitting in a rather small room, watching a man lying on a couch and talking in his "sleep," while a stenographer jots down his words. Suppose this sleeping man has just told you that you once lived, more than 29,000 years ago, in a society which in many ways was more advanced than the one you're living in today. Incredibly, this sleeping man has just said that you were "in the Atlantean land at the time of development of electrical forces that dealt with transportation of craft from place to place, photographing at a distance, reading inscriptions through walls even at a distance, overcoming gravity itself, preparation of the crystal, the terrible mighty crystal. Much of this brought destruction."

Would you believe this sleeping man? Probably not. You might even think he had taken leave of his senses—unconscious or otherwise.

You might think this, unless you later compared what Edgar Cayce had said about *your* experiences on the legendary continent of Atlantis with what he had said about the experiences of others, and found that, regardless of the number of years separating the readings, all the experiences meshed together to make a cohesive and fascinating whole, a compelling argument for the *reality* of Atlantis! Then you would be left to wonder. . . .

Hugh Lynn Cayce, in the Preface to another book in this series, *Edgar Cayce on Atlantis,* written by Edgar Evans Cayce, discussed this perplexing subject. "My brother, the author, and I know that Edgar Cayce did not read Plato's material on Atlantis, or books on Atlantis, and that he, so far as we know, had absolutely no knowledge of this subject. If his unconscious fabricated this material or wove it together from existing legends and writings, we believe that it is the most amazing example of a telepathic-clairvoyant scanning of existing legends and stories in print or of the minds of persons dealing with the Atlantis theory. As my brother and I have said from time to time, life would be simpler if Edgar Cayce had never mentioned Atlantis."

However, Edgar Cayce did mention Atlantis. Of the 2,500 life readings on file at A.R.E., at least 30 percent contain references to previous incarnations on this lost continent.

Unfortunately, few dates concerning Atlantis appear in the readings. This is because few were requested, and few were volunteered by the sleeping Cayce. However, enough were given that it has been possible to pull together a chronologically consistent picture of this ancient land and its people.

He described the location of the lost Atlantis as lying "between the Gulf of Mexico on one side and the Mediterranean on the other. Evidences of Atlantean civilization," he said, "may be found in the Pyrenees and Morocco and in British Honduras, Yucatan and parts of the Americas—especially near Bimini and in the Gulf Stream, in this vicinity."

Roughly, the three distinct periods in the history of Atlantis described by Cayce break down into three eras marked by destruction of part of the land: around 50,000 B.C., around 28,000 B.C., and the final, complete sinking under the sea between the years 10,500 and 10,000 B.C. This latter period was one of gradual disappearance over some 7,500 years until, finally, Atlantis was no more.

The man inhabiting Atlantis, said Cayce, was of the red race. Asked in November, 1932, to elaborate on the origin, of the five races, Cayce stated that they had come into existence simultaneously. Where? "As we find—those in the Gobi the yellow, the white in the Carpathians, the red in the Atlantean and in the American, the brown in the Andean, the black in the plain and the Sudan or in the African."

Many readings on file discuss incarnations in Atlantis prior to 50,000 B.C. It was a time of friction between two groups: those who represented good (Cayce called them the "children of the Law of One") and those who were evil (called "the Sons of Belial"). Their warring led eventually to destruction of a portion of the continent.

Concerning this awful time, Cayce once said, "There were those who questioned the expedience of acquainting the workers with applications of material and spiritual laws—saw divine and spiritual laws become destructive. For when the facets were prepared for the motivative forces from the rays of the sun to be effective upon those ships and electrical forces, when these were turned upon the elements of the earth, the first upheavals occurred."

In another reading, he said, ". . . in the Atlantean land during the period of the first destruction or separation of land . . . [the entity] aided in the preparation of explosives or those things that set in motion the fires of the inner portion of the earth."

Is it possible that there was a civilization prior to 50,000 B.C. so advanced that solar rays were controlled and directed at one's enemies with a force powerful enough to trigger volcanic eruptions? Is it *possible*?

Another living in that same time, Cayce stated, was "in the Atlantean land just preceding the first breaking up of the land, when there was the use of those influences *that are again being discovered* [Author's italics]—that may be used for benefits in communications, transportation, etc., or turned into destructive forces." This reading was given in May, 1941. On December 2, 1942, the first sustained controlled production of atomic energy was accomplished.

This was not an isolated case. There were many others, given over a number of years, that supplied the same general information—with variations, but never at variance with each other.

Here's an excerpt from another reading, in 1933: "In Atlantis the entity attended the meeting of many representatives of many countries to devise ways of dealing with the great animals overrunning the earth. Means were devised to change environs suitable for beasts. This was administered by sending out death rays or super cosmic rays from various central plants. *These rays will be discovered within the next twenty-five years.*" [Author's italics.] Cayce, answering a question concerning the date of this meeting, said that the year was 50,722 B.C.

Adding twenty-five years to the date of this 1933 reading would place the time of discovery of such rays at 1958. In 1955, the antiproton was discovered. Out of this came the discovery, in 1957, of the antineutron. Thus we had, by 1958, the theoretical possibility, through the combination—in principal—of antiprotons and antineutrons which would form "antimatter." Should antimatter come into contact with ordinary matter, all its mass would be converted into energy, rather than the fraction of it as in the case of nuclear fission and fusion reactions.

Another scientific advance in 1958 seems to be in line

with the prophecy in this reading: the development of a workable maser—short for "microwave amplification by stimulated emission of radiation." Amplification is accomplished as a result of storing up energy in a small insulating crystal of special magnetic properties. An incident signal triggers off the release of energy, and the crystal passes on more energy than it has taken in.

Since that time, the maser has been considerably developed. The same is true of the laser—which stands for "light amplification by stimulated emission of radiation"; in other words, an optical maser. It, too, was developed in 1958.

There are a number of Cayce readings which refer to the use of crystals that sound suspiciously like a type of maser or laser. These mentions were most often found in connection with incarnations in Atlantis during the second period, ending with the destruction in 28,000 B.C., and the third period, ending with the final destruction in 10,000 B.C.

Concerning what life in Atlantis was like around the year 28,000 B.C., Cayce had this to say in a reading for an individual: "In the Atlantean land before the second destruction, when there was the dividing of the islands, the entity was among those that interpreted the messages received through the crystal and the fires that were to be the eternal fires of nature. New developments in air and water travel are no surprise to the entity, as these were beginning development at that period."

Another individual, he said, had been "in Atlantis when there were those activities which later brought about the second upheaval in the land. The entity was what would be in the present the electrical engineer, [and] applied those forces or influences for aircraft, ships and what you would today call radio in a form for constructive or destructive purposes."

Still another individual, Cayce said, "was associated with those who dealt with mechanical appliances and their application, during the experience. And as we find, it was a period when there was much that has not even been thought of yet, in the present experience."

In 1933, Cayce gave a long description of technological

206

developments in Atlantis, together with elaborate instructions for construction of the building which housed the "firestone," or crystal, mentioned earlier. According to the reading, it was this crystal which, through "unintentionally being set too high," had caused the second destruction in Atlantis' and had broken up the land into islands which eventually led to the final sinking.

Said Cayce of this crystal, "The records as to ways of constructing same are in three places in the earth, as it stands today: in the sunken portion of Atlantis, or Poseidia, where a portion of the temples may yet be discovered under the slime of ages of sea water—near what is known as Bimini, off the coast of Florida. And, secondly, in the temple records that were in Egypt, where the entity acted later in cooperation with others towards preserving the records that came from the land where these had been kept. Also, thirdly, the records that were carried to what is now Yucatan, in America, where these stones (which they know so little about) are now—during the last few months—being uncovered.

"In Yucatan there is the emblem of same. Let's clarify this, for it may be more easily found. For they will be brought to this America, these United States. A portion is to be carried, as we find, to the Pennsylvania State Museum. A portion is to be carried to the Washington preservations of such findings; or to Chicago."

Cayce was unquestionably correct in saying that too little was known of these stones—drawings or carvings of which, possibly from some temple, he said were being uncovered at the time of his 1933 reading. At any rate, if they were discovered they have yet to be identified and announced by any archaeologist or museum.

The third and final destruction of Atlantis, of what remained of the islands, took place during the period between 10,500 and 10,000 B.C. Edgar Evans Cayce has speculated that this may be the portion alluded to by Plato. Approximately 50 percent of the life readings which mention Atlantis incarnations are concerned with this era, and with the parallel activities in pre-history Egypt.

The readings indicate that many of the people who fled

the sinking Atlantis islands went to Egypt; others to the Pyrenees, or to Europe, Africa, and even to the Americas.

Perhaps it is in Egypt that the full story of Atlantis may someday be uncovered. For, said Cayce, copies of all the important documents and records dealing with the history of the lost continent and its civilization were taken to Egypt by fleeing Atlanteans, and were eventually placed in the Hall of Records, a small tomb or pyramid which lies between the right paw of the Sphinx and the Nile River. This enclosure also contains the bodies of many of the Atlanteans who brought these materials to Egypt, said Cayce, as well as a number of artifacts which will verify the former existence of Atlantis. There will be found, when the Hall of Records is uncovered, musical instruments, "the hangings, the accoutrements for the altar in the temple of the day," plaques and life seals, surgical instruments and medical compounds, gold and precious stones, linens. All that remains is for us to *find* the Hall of Records!

Of course, we may not have to wait much longer for some sign of the former existence of this strange continent. On June 28, 1940, the sleeping Cayce made this startling statement. "Poseidia will be among the first portions of Atlantis to rise again. Expect it in '68 and '69—not so far away!" The second of the three sacred temples, holding the secrets of Atlantis, was said to be there.

Or we may find the answer to some of the mysteries surrounding Atlantis in Yucatan. There, said Cayce in a reading in 1933, will be found the Temple of Iltar, the third of the spots in which the Atlantis records were placed. (The readings state that the people who migrated there from Atlantis came not only by ship, but by air!) Cayce once discussed the fate of Iltar's people. "Those in Yucatan, those in the adjoining lands as begun by Iltar, gradually lost in their activities (through generations) and came to be that people termed, in other portions of America, the Mound Builders."

According to Cayce, there are many secrets still to be disclosed within The Great Pyramid of Gizeh, the oldest pyramid in Egypt and the one closest to the Nile. It is generally assumed to have been built around 2885 B.C.

Cayce, however, stated that it was built in the one hundred years between 10,490 to 10,390 B.C., and that the Sphinx was constructed around the same time.

We find some clues to their construction in a portion of a reading for an individual who, according to Cayce, had helped to build the Sphinx. "As the monuments were being rebuilt in the plains of that now called the Pyramid of Gizeh," he said, "this entity builded, laid, the foundations. That is, supervised same, figured out the geometrical position of same as [in] relation to those buildings as were put up of that connecting the Sphinx, and the data concerning same may be found in the vaults in the base of the Sphinx. The entity was with that dynasty . . . when these buildings [were] begun. This laid out, base of Sphinx, in channels, and in the corner facing the Gizeh may be found that of the wording of how this was founded, giving the history . . ."

Information concerning the Sphinx, said Cayce, would be found "in the base of the left forearm, or leg, of the prostrate beast, in the base of foundation. Not in the underground channel—as was opened by the ruler many years, many centuries, later—but in the real base, or that as would be termed in the present parlance as the cornerstone. . . ."

Within the Pyramid of Gizeh, he said, would be found all the information dealing with the period in which great advances were made in pre-history Egypt, following the migration from Atlantis of a people more advanced than those in Egypt in that era. But that's not all. The information in Gizeh concerns not only pre-history Egypt; it covers *the entire history of mankind from that time until the year 1998*—which is, said Cayce, "that period when there is to be the change in the earth's position, and the return of the Great Initiate to that and other lands, for the fulfillment of those prophecies depicted there.

"All changes that occurred in the religious thought in the world are shown there: in the variations in which the passage through same is reached, from the base to the top—or to the open tomb and the top. These [changes] are signified both by the layer and the color and the direction of the turn."

Cayce, in his readings, often referred to The Great

Pyramid as the "Pyramid of Understanding." Built as a hall of initiation—through the process of levitation, "by those universal laws and forces of nature which cause iron to float," Cayce explained—it served as the "House Initiate" for those dedicating themselves to special services in the secrets of the mystery religion of Egypt. Here the masters performed their vows, consecrating themselves to holy service. It had a much higher purpose, then, than that of a burial place.

Within the Great Pyramid, say the readings, is a record in stone of the history and development of man from the time of Araaraat (the King) and Ra (the High Priest: Cayce in an earlier incarnation, during which he was also known as Ra Ta) to the end of the present earth cycle, or 1998. Its records are written in the language of mathematics, geometry and astronomy, as well as in the kinds of stone used, with their symbology. At the end of the cycle, there is to be another change in the earth's position (generally taken to mean a shifting of the poles) and the return of the Great Initiate for the culmination of the prophecies. All changes that have come and are to come, said Cayce, are shown there in the passages from the base to the top. Changes are signified by the layer of stone, the color of it, and the direction in which the turns are made. Thus the real message of the Great Pyramid, according to Cayce, is in code; there are no undiscovered rooms, as such, there.

The smaller pyramid, the Hall of Records still covered by sand, does contain a sealed room. The readings describe it as a vault sealed with heavy metal, and state that, among other things, it contains the prophecy for the period from 1958 to 1998!

Prophecy: What Lies Ahead?

In the first chapter of this book, we mentioned some of the Cayce prophecies that have been proved by the passage of time. These have been covered completely in other books, together with prophecies for the future years: notably, in Jess Stearn's *Edgar Cayce—The Sleeping Prophet,* and Mary Ellen Carter's *Edgar Cayce on Prophecy.*

Naturally enough, it is the Cayce prophecies concerning

earth changes which have garnered the most public attention, particularly those predicted for the period 1958 to 1998. They are literally earth-shaking, and should they come true would affect great numbers of people.

I think it is right that these should be noticed, because I feel there was some purpose, probably a great one, in Cayce's giving them to us.

But I will not list them here. Space does not permit my discussing them adequately, and anything short of that, I think, would be irresponsible. Instead, I would suggest that the reader get the full information from the above-listed books, as well as from a booklet published by A.R.E. entitled "Earth Changes."

I do, however, have one point—a personal one—to make. The Cayce prophecy concerning the future destruction of Los Angeles, San Francisco and New York City has caused me much anxiety, for I happen to live just a few miles south of San Francisco. Common sense tells me that, living as I do on the very edge of one of America's most active faults, the San Andreas, my chances of being caught up in the massive destruction—predicted by Cayce to occur within the years 1958 to 1998—are quite good. Geologists tell us that, as far as severe earthquakes are concerned, our area is overdue for at least one—and that it can occur ten minutes or ten years from now. And yet building heights continue to rise, and power plants and communications centers and schools and public buildings continue to be built *directly along the line of the fault!* I need no psychic to tell me that I am living on top of a time bomb.

But I must admit that my first reaction, upon hearing about Cayce's prophecy, was to consider the possibility of moving away. I thought about it quite a lot.

And then it occurred to me that it was not the threat of sudden death that disturbed me—it was the idea that my home and everything in it might be destroyed, and that I'd have to start all over again, building from the ruins.

This is an unpleasant admission, even to oneself, for it reflects the one human failing above all others that Edgar Cayce in his readings was trying to get across to us: our tendency to let the material side of life govern the spiritual. In one reading, he put it this way: "These ex-

211

periences, then, that have shattered hopes, that have brought disappointment, that have produced periods when there seemed little or nothing left in material life—if they are used as stepping stones and not as those things that bring resentment, accusation of others, discontent, we will find they will become helpful experiences that may guide one into a haven that is quiet and peaceful."

CHAPTER FOURTEEN

DREAMS

Of the more than 14,000 psychic readings in the Cayce files, approximately 1,000 deal in some way with the most personal activity of the human mind: the process of dreaming.

Some of these readings were given in order to advance our general knowledge of what happens when we surrender ourselves to sleep. Some were given for the purpose of interpreting the dreams of others. And some were devoted to interpretation of Edgar Cayce's own dreams.

It was in October, 1923, that Cayce first described the subject. "As in dream, those forces of the subconscious when taken as correlated with those [dream] forms that relate to the various phases of the individual, give to that individual a better understanding of self, when correctly interpreted, or when correctly answered.

"Forget not that it has been said correctly that the Creator, the gods and the God of the Universe, speak to man through his individual self. Man approaches the more intimate conditions of that field of the inner self when the conscious [self] is at rest in sleep or slumber, at which time more of the inner forces are taken into consideration and studied by the individual, and not someone else. It is each individual's job, if he will study to show himself approved (by God, his Maker) to understand his individual condition, his individual position in relation to others, his individual manifestation, through his individual receiving of messages from the higher forces themselves (thus, through dreams).

"In this age—at present 1923—there is not sufficient credence given dreams; for the best development of the human family is to give the greater increase in knowledge of the subconscious soul or spirit world."

Perhaps we should restate, here, the human mind as it was described in the readings. The conscious mind, said Cayce, is that which has to do with the activities of the physical body. The subconscious mind is that of the soul;

and the readings emphasize that the more authority given to the unconscious, the more creative and useful work it is able to do. The superconscious mind, that term which infuriates so many literal-minded men of science, is the mind of the spirit—that part of us which is attuned to the forces of God.

Immediately after the series of "sleep" readings given by Cayce in 1923, a number of people closely associated with his work began to record their dreams and bring them to him for interpretation through his psychic source. This led to a most interesting discovery: it is possible, through concentration and practice, to greatly increase our awareness of dreams, as well as our ability to remember them long enough to get them recorded. The dreams, and their interpretations, were closely studied, and a good deal of information came out of this informal "Cayce sleep laboratory."

In 1932, Cayce was asked in a reading to "outline clearly and comprehensively the material which should be presented to the general public in explaining just what occurs in the conscious, subconscious, and spiritual forces of an entity while in the state known as sleep."

He answered, "Yes. While a great deal has been written and spoken regarding the experiences of individuals in that state called sleep, only recently has there been the attempt to control it or form any definite idea of what produces conditions in the unconscious, subconscious, subliminal or subnormal mind. These attempts have been to produce—or to determine that which produces—the kinds of dreams experienced by an individual entity.

"For some minds such experiments may determine questions respecting the claim of some psychiatrist or psychoanalyst. Such experiments may refute or determine the value of such claims in the study of certain kinds of mental disturbances in individuals. Yet little of this can be called a true analysis of what really happens to the body—either physical, mental, subconscious or spiritual—when it loses itself in such repose.

"There are certain definite conditions, to be sure, which take place respecting the physical, the conscious, and the subconscious, as well as the spiritual forces of the body."

That reading, of course, was in the early 'thirties, long

before the discoveries about sleep and dreaming that have come—only within the past decade—as a result of sleep laboratories utilizing the most sophisticated electronic equipment available.

The experiments mentioned by Cayce might well have referred to those being conducted, around the time of the reading, by the foremost pioneer in sleep research, Dr. Nathaniel Kleitman, a professor of physiology at the University of Chicago. An interesting point of conjecture is that at that time Kleitman was only at the threshold of his work, for he was approaching it from a physiological standpoint alone, studying the physical processes of sleep. Another twenty years were to pass before Kleitman would recognize the physical processes of *dreaming,* when he noticed that the eyes of all individuals continue to flutter beneath their lids after all signs of consciousness have passed. It was from this base that the modern sleep laboratory was built. And from this laboratory has come solid proof that *everyone* dreams.

On a typical night of sleeping, a person has four or five dreams—the first beginning about 90 minutes after sleep has come. Of these, the first dreams are short; later ones are more extended. The fluttering of the eyes, called "rapid eye movements," correspond to periods of dreaming. While outwardly the body may seem completely calm, the process of dreaming brings inner tumult for the physical body, involving changes in heartbeat, breathing, secretion of hormones and gastric juices, and so forth. The brain undergoes measurable changes, and at times seems even more active than in some states of wakefulness (such as while listening to the radio.) Brain temperature increases slightly, and the rate of metabolism in the brain seems to indicate that tremendous amounts of energy are being expended while dreaming.

These, of course, are the physiological signs of dreaming. They are extremely important, for out of the laboratory may come scientific establishment of what Cayce discussed in his readings many years ago: the significance of dreams, and their involvement with the *sixth sense!*

Cayce stated it this way, in excerpts from a series of sleep readings given in 1932:

"First, we would say, sleep is a shadow of that intermission in the earth's experiences—that state called death. For physical consciousness becomes unaware of existent conditions in sleep, save as attributes of the physical partake of attributes of the imaginative, or the subconscious and unconscious forces of the same body. That is, in a normal sleep (from the physical standpoint we are reasoning now) the senses are on guard, so to speak, so that the auditory forces are the ones which are more sensitive. . . .

"So, then, we find that there are what is ordinarily known as four other senses, acting independently but coordinating in awareness, for the physical body to be conscious. These four, in the state of sleep or repose, or rest, or exhaustion (and when induced by any influence from the outside) have become unaware of that which is taking place about the individual so resting. . . ."

With the "relaxation" of the four senses of taste, touch, sight and smell, say the readings, comes a division of the sense of hearing. This one sense, during sleep, functions in place of the five conscious senses, and does something more: it creates a sixth sense which is capable of a whole new activity.

This activity was described by Cayce in another reading. "There is an active force within each individual which functions in the manner of a sense when the body-physical is in sleep, repose or rest. We would outline what are the functions of this thing we have chosen to call a sixth sense.

"This sixth sense activity is the activating force or power of the other self. What other self? That which has been builded by the entity or body, or soul, throughout all its experiences as a whole, in the material and cosmic world, see? It may be termed a faculty of the soul-body itself."

Cayce elaborated on this. "Sleep is that period of time when the soul takes stock of what it has acted upon from one rest period to another; drawing comparisons—as it were—which comprise life itself, in its essence.

"In sleep all things become possible. One finds himself flying through space, or being pursued . . . by those very components which make for comparisons with what has been builded by the very soul of the body itself."

Among those who brought their dreams to the sleeping Cayce for interpretation were some who seemed to have a good deal of psychic awareness, possibly even a talent for prophecy as it came to them through their dreaming.

One often-reported case is that of a young woman who dreamed, soon after her marriage, of the birth of a weak-minded baby. Cayce's interpretation of the dream indicated that it might well be a warning of things to come. The child who was born two years later seemed perfectly healthy and normal. However, at the age of twenty-five he was committed to a mental institution.

Had this been an isolated instance in the life of this young woman, we might toss it off as coincidence, or even as the result of marital difficulties, divorce and all manner of unpleasant occurrences in her family life, for certainly her son must have been affected by these things. However, she had a total of eighty-five dreams interpreted by Edgar Cayce between the years 1925 and 1930, and a number of them seem to indicate some telepathic, even precognitive ability.

In December, 1926, for example, she mentioned one dream in which her friend, Emmie, had committed suicide. Cayce's interpretation of this was, "This shows to the entity, through this correlation of mental forces of the body-mind itself and those of the body-mind of Emmie, that such conditions had passed through this mind—or had contemplated such conditions, see? They have passed."

The dreamer had not been in touch with Emmie for several years. She wrote to her and learned that Emmie had, indeed, contemplated suicide around the time of the dream, but had since managed to get into a better frame of mind.

Cayce was asked to explain how the information about Emmie had come through the dream. He first gave an outline of the various types of dreams: nightmares, resulting from physical discomforts; symbolic dreams; problem solving; and psychic dreams. The dream about Emmie, said Cayce, had been a psychic one. He explained, "Others there are, a correlation between mentalities or subconscious entities, wherein there has been attained, physically or mentally, a correlation of individual ideas or

217

mental expressions, that bring from one subconscious to another those of actual existent conditions, either direct or indirect, to be acted upon or that are ever present, see?

"Hence we find visions of the past, visions of the present, visions of the future. For the subconscious there is no past or future—all is present. This would be well to remember in much of the information as may be given through such forces as these."

In the A.R.E. booklet, "Dreams: The Language of the Unconscious," there is an article by Tom C. Clark dealing with his study of the readings in which ninety-one of Edgar Cayce's own dreams were interpreted, between January, 1925 and February, 1940. There were many curious circumstances involved in these readings.

First, there was the matter of eleven dreams experienced by Edgar Cayce while he was in the self-induced sleep necessary to give a reading for someone else! It is almost impossible to accept the complexity of a situation in which Edgar Cayce, at his home in Virginia Beach and reading for someone, say, in New York City, might suddenly become aware of the fact that he was not only getting the information requested for the reading, but was dreaming his own dream as well! Even more puzzling, he would remember the dream afterwards, but as usual would have no recollection whatsoever about the subject of the reading.

That even so talented a psychic as Edgar Cayce might have trouble living up to the messages received in his readings is difficult to imagine. And yet, after examining Cayce's early readings in which he interpreted his own dreams, Mr. Clark had this to say. "In the early dreams between 1925 and 1930, Cayce is revealed as struggling and fighting with himself. He had a premonition that what came through him was of a divine nature and his dreams revealed to him that he was anything but a divine individual. He struggled desperately with himself to live by and bring into his conscious life a few divine principles. At one time his psychic source, when asked to interpret a dream, refused the information because, it said, in the past, in connection with similar dreams which had been interpreted, Edgar Cayce had ignored the lesson and done nothing in his life to make correction or adjustment. Even

218

his psychic informant, then, turned against him with impatience and criticism. In certain respects—and unfortunately they were important—he was a weak man, even as most of us in these respects are weak.

"After 1932, the content of the dreams started to alter. Fewer dreams were submitted to the psychic source for interpretation and there was evident a definite change in Edgar Cayce's spiritual development. The conflicts and doubts were pretty well resolved and he had a clearer intuitive comprehension of the meaning, importance, and validity of the information which came through him."

This would seem to provide a striking example of the way an individual, any individual, may profit from an understanding of what his dreams may mean.

Lacking an Edgar Cayce to interpret our dreams, however, what chance do we have of learning to understand them? Well, our first step must be to become aware of them.

Experiments conducted several years ago by A.R.E., working with a group of volunteers, showed that this is more easily accomplished than one might think. People who reported, the first week, that they had not dreamed at all were reporting, by the third week, not only the types of dreams brought on by physical conditions and surroundings, but even those in which some psychic source seemed evident.

In discussing this with Hugh Lynn Cayce some months ago, I mentioned my own problem—a not unusual one. I explained that I have many dreams during the night, but generally cannot hold on to them, during the process of waking up (a slow and painful ordeal for me) long enough for my conscious mind to grab on to them.

He suggested that I do as his volunteers had done: place a pad and pencil on the night stand, and form the habit of jotting down my dreams even before coming completely awake. Then I explained that my mind wakes up before my body does, so that by the time I could get my writing arm in action, the dream would be gone. He made a simple and logical suggestion: that I place a tape recorder beside the bed.

Feeling slightly foolish at first, I did just that. My early attempts gave me little more than gibberish, but by the end of about ten days I found myself doing a fairly efficient job of it. Now I've progessed a step further; generally, I simply transfer the dream directly to my conscious mind and find that, by just thinking out the dream in this way, I can retain it. I've been amazed by the number of prophetic dreams I've experienced in the past several months—some purely personal, and many on a national or international scale. I've also solved some real problems by saying, before going to sleep, that they will be worked out during the night while I'm "resting."

Which brings up the other major suggestion given to me by Hugh Lynn Cayce. That is, several times before dropping off to sleep, I say to myself, "I will recall what I dream." No doubt this mechanism is as simple as it seems; that it's merely a matter of making the conscious mind aware of the importance of the dream, and thus receptive to it.

But once awareness, and memory, of a dream are achieved, what does the dream mean? This is where things get a bit more complicated—though not impossible.

Many dreams can be easily explained by physical conditions (the body or the surroundings); or by events going on in the person's life which are continued on into the dream world. Probably the majority of dreams fall into this category.

Others are clothed in symbolism, and in order to understand them we must understand the symbols. But not all symbols are the same for all people—although once established for the individual, they generally remain constant.

The following list, then, is not meant to apply to each individual, but merely to supply the sort of pattern that symbols will be found to make. These are the symbols that have been taken from the Cayce readings as being most universal in nature:

Water—Source of life, spirit, unconscious
Boat—Voyage of life
Explosion—Turmoils
Fire—Wrath, cleansing, destroying
A Person—Represents what the dreamer feels toward that person

Clothing—The way one appears to others

Animals—Represent some phase of self, according to what one feels about the animal seen. In this area especially the universal, historical and racial quality of meaning must be considered. For example, the bull, sexless human figure, lion and eagle may for many persons symbolize the four lower vital centers of the body; the sex glands, cells of Leydig, adrenals, and thymus, in that order. The snake is both a wisdom symbol and a sex symbol, associated with the kundalini. When raised to the higher centers in the head it becomes the wisdom symbol.

Fish—Christ, Christian, spiritual food

Dead Leaves—Body drosses

Mud, Mire, Tangled Weeds—That which needs cleansing

Naked—Open to criticism, exposed

This list is intended to serve only as a starting point. The person who records his dreams for a few weeks will see a general pattern emerging. Certain symbols will be seen to recur in such a way that their meaning will soon become clear—at which time the individual's own list of symbols can be compiled.

Whether or not a dreamer goes so far as to develop a list of symbols, however, he'll find it interesting to begin to "listen" to what his unconscious mind, speaking the language of dreams, has to say to him.

For, through dreaming, we have the most natural, and certainly the safest, bridge to a part of the mind that is hidden from a waking world. It can tell us a good deal about our emotions, our physical health, our talents, our failings, and even—with practice in understanding its messages—a great deal about the psychic and spiritual sides of our being.

CHAPTER FIFTEEN

CONCLUSION

I grew up at Virginia Beach, during the years in which Cayce lived and worked there. I thought I knew him. But I have only truly come to know him through study of his psychic readings.

The modest, humble man who was my friend and neighbor was only part of the story; just as this book is only part of the story. But I was a child when I knew him, and was still a child when he died. Although I knew that he did strange, wonderful things when he "went to sleep," it was not this part of Edgar Cayce that I knew. The man I knew grew the largest, juiciest strawberries I had ever seen, and certainly the sweetest I had ever tasted. The man I knew was a quiet man, and I was surprised to learn, only a few years ago, that he had a terrible temper at times that bothered him more than it bothered anybody else, for I never saw a sign of temper in him. The man I knew was towering-tall, laughed often, and had an ability to communicate with children that is given to few men.

I was too young to understand the depth of the man, or the depth of the matters of which he spoke while asleep. I knew that through his readings he was able to bring health back to ailing bodies, for I had seen such "miracles" performed for members of my own family. I was wise enough to know that he did not tell fortunes; but not wise enough to know that the life reading that would have been given for me, had I accepted it when it was offered, would have helped me find my real work in life much earlier than the age of thirty-six, and possibly to avoid some of the more serious mistakes of my life—or at least to understand why I made them!

Since I didn't have my own life reading, then, I've had to find my own benefits in the readings through studying those given for others. The benefits have been many, and the pleasures too numerous to mention.

Serious study of the readings has brought me—through its complete involvement with matters concerning the human body, the human mind, and the human spirit—to a new awareness of man's real purpose in the earth. Concentration on the vast scope, the universal nature of the Cayce readings, dealing as they do with past, present and future, has broadened my respect for this most talented of all psychics.

It seems to me, as I look back over the great number of readings I studied for the purpose of this effort—far too many of which were excluded for one reason alone: a lack of space—that there is enough material here to keep thousands of researchers busy for at least another century. Where there is so much still to be learned about the workings of the human body and the human mind, I cannot help believing that many of the ultimate answers may well be found within the readings. As has been said, some research is now being conducted along these lines—but surely there is much more that could be done, *should* be done.

That some of the methods of treatment seem clumsy by today's standards should not deter doctors of medicine, and doctors of psychology, from examining what Cayce had to say. As long as there are the tragedies of multiple sclerosis, arthritis, cancer, schizophrenia, drug addiction and other ills plaguing mankind, does orthodox medicine have a right to close the door on the possibility that Cayce was giving the true answers to these problems? Does the psychiatrist have a right to refuse to consider that man may have lived before, and that the reason he acts the way he does may be at least partially due to past experiences of other lifetimes?

As a child, I often heard the phrase used in connection with Cayce's work, "first for the few; then for the masses." This phrase had come directly from the readings, to indicate that Cayce's readings would apply, first, to the individual; would then be studied in small groups; and finally would be explained to the general public. I understood this, or thought I did.

At the same time, I wondered why so many people thought of Mr. Cayce as a strange man who did strange things, and why so many people said they did not believe in the things they'd heard about him. I heard stories about people who came—sometimes several at a time—to show him up as a fake, a charlatan. I knew that these people always went away saying things like, "I don't know what it is he does; but it certainly seems to work."

Now, from the vantage point of my middle years, I think I understand it all a bit better. I am still dismayed that so many people of science will slam the door on any investigation into psychic phenomena in general, or Edgar Cayce's work in particular, for it seems to me that we accept all sorts of things as possible, even if we can't explain them fully. Electricity, for one. The miracle of conception and birth, for another. These things have no business working, but they do. The Cayce readings worked, too, even if we don't know quite how, and why, they did.

I used to wonder why Cayce was a man of *this* particular century, rather than the next, which might be somewhat more willing to accept and *use* the information he had to offer. But I look at man today, with all his faults; and then I look at man's ideal, as shown in the readings, and it seems to me that if there was ever a century for Edgar Cayce, this is the one! If we ever needed an understanding of man's purpose in the earth, and a reiteration of the spiritual values that must guide his steps as he strives to make sure that there will be a next century, then this, most certainly, is the time!

For the focus in the readings is on the individual. It is for the individual, by understanding himself and his fellow man, to find his own reason for existing, to shape his own destiny—with the help of a living God.

At a time when we are being more and more computerized, more and more made a part of a don't-staple-or-mutilate-this-card society, it is good to be reminded that we are, after all, individuals. And that what we do as individuals—as individual souls—goes to make up the story of mankind. We can change the world, or we can destroy it.